ARMAGEDDON'S
WAR
ON THE MIND

IS THE BATTLE OF
ARMAGEDDON IN YOUR MIND?

Armando Herrera

Armageddon's War on the Mind

Trilogy Christian Publishers A Wholly Owned Subsidiary of Trinity Broadcasting Network

2442 Michelle Drive Tustin, CA 92780

Manufactured in the United States of America

10 9 8 7 6 5 4 3 2 1

Library of Congress Cataloging-in-Publication Data is available.

ISBN: 978-1-68556-056-0

E-ISBN: 978-1-68556-057-7

TABLE OF CONTENTS

FOREWORD

God has given us what we need to live well. To name a few, we have the Holy Spirit, the Word of God, and the cross of the risen Savior to communicate His many provisions. These resources share the exact divine origin. When establishing the value of each unique Godly resolve, I will often repeat the attributes of God's provisions relative to their ability to keep hell at bay. I choose to do this rather than compromise the clarity each subject deserves. In doing so, I could provoke the readers' reproaches, but I would rather the writer suffer than this work's content.

PREFACE

In the summer of 73, I went with a friend to my first Bible study. It was in Southern California in a town called Pasadena. I was not religious but agreed to go because of my friend's persistence. Walking into the house when we arrived, I realized the only time I had been in a home with this many young people was at the wild parties I used to attend. All the people at this party were sober and delightful. After thirty minutes of introductions, we were getting in a big circle and holding hands, ready to pray. All of this seemed strange to me. But somehow, I felt these strangers cared for me—something I had never experienced before. After the prayer started, one girl in the group collapsed to the ground. She seemed lifeless, almost dead. People huddled around her, and then a couple of guys and gals carried her motionless body into one of the back bedrooms. I did not know what to think.

Everybody prayed quietly. After about ten minutes, the most horrific of sounds began coming from the back bedroom. I realized this girl was screaming uncontrollably, and I could hear the people in the room praying for her. I was freaking out. After thirty minutes of constant loud prayers and shouting coming from the back room, it stopped. They came out with the girl, who seemed calm and very peaceful. My first experience with Christianity was seeing a demon-possessed girl fighting for her freedom. When I got home, I remember frantically telling my parents that God and Jesus were real. They asked me how I knew, and I told them the Devil showed me. It perplexed them. Partly because before that night, I had nothing to do with religion. So before my journey with Jesus Christ began at the first Bible study I ever attended, I saw how the invisible realm impacts peoples' lives and saw firsthand how the netherworld operates.

INTRODUCTION:

THE FAMILY OF GOD

To use a traditional phrase from the halls of humanity, "God is a family man." Of course, in today's vernacular, we convey this truth by saying God loves being a part of a family. However you define it, like us, God is into having a relationship with those He dearly loves. The Father, Son, and divine Spirit, though uniquely separate individuals, are one. Collectively, they are God. Their relationship with each other is so unique that it moved them to share this "family" environment encompassing their eternal dwelling. They wanted to have a social unit outside of themselves to share the fantastic reality of their existence.

They used their creative powers to make living beings. Initially, they created a divine family. After which, they started a terrestrial one. However, like you and me, these created individuals could choose to be a part of God's family or decide to live according to their desires separate from God. First, part of the divine family rebelled and broke away from God's eternal plan of creation. Then, the rebellion of the terrestrial family followed. However, free will cannot prohibit God from having the loving relationship He intends for those He created. Ultimately, for those who choose God's plan, both divine and terrestrial, God's intended purpose for His created beings will become a reality. Despite the resistance towards this end, nothing in all the design will stop God from having an eternal family.

CHAPTER 1:

CHRIST IS KING

First Corinthians 15:14 says, "And if Christ has not risen, then our preaching is empty, and your faith is also empty."

Paul, the apostle, wrote these remarks after the crucifixion of Jesus Christ. I am referencing this text because, if Christ is not alive, this work's topic is likewise empty. I devised this work to shed light on the effects the unseen world has on this natural realm. It describes the phenomenon of sacred combat. Jesus Christ is the sole authority capable of preventing Satan from obtaining control of our modes of living. The power of the cross and the news of the truth is God unveiled to humanity. God has shown us how to overthrow the efforts of darkness in our forms of living. Since the downfall of man in the garden of Eden, Satan has had a death grip on humanity. Through the cross, Jesus took the keys of death and hell out of the Devil's grips and has levied a death blow on him (Revelation 1:18). Satan's eternal fate is unchangeable. Humanity's future is not. Because of this, it outrages Satan. He is livid with God and His human beings. He seeks to exterminate us. Every individual's destiny is at stake. There is a war going on between light and darkness. The prize that goes to the victor of this war is your heart. God yearns to free your life. Satan desires to abduct it. Satan knows God possesses a strategy of escape for humans. There is a perpetual struggle for the souls of every individual living. Hell intends to eradicate as many lives as imaginable. Beyond the intent to inflict suffering in life, Satan wants as many individuals as possible with him in internal torment. The Bible declares that Jesus Christ is the way, the truth, and the life (John 14:6). His living example showed how to break hell's effect in our way of life and provided the opportunity for us to spend eternity in the presence of loving Father God. Satan is an actual being; God exists; Jesus Christ ascended from the dead.

Ignorance of these facts is not bliss. The actual truth is infinite. It has always existed and will forever continue. We must come to understand the power struggle in the unseen netherworld to find out why certain events occur in this temporal physical reality. My prayer is that through revelation and relationship, the Holy Spirit will inspire many to search out the scriptures relative to the ever-present battle for human beings' lives. God is infinite in power yet all benevolent. Those who approach the throne of God must recognize it as holy ground. God is to remain preeminent among all the nations.

First Corinthians 15:19 says, "If in this life only we have hope in Christ, we are of all men the most pitiable."

If this ordinary human experience is everything existence comprises, we will someday cease to exist. Suppose who we currently are is all we have to look forward to, and there is no future eternal salvation expectation. If that is the case, every person who emphasizes this life's concerns is much wiser than the Christian who puts their faith in Jesus Christ. Faith is deficient if the prize of that hope is not more significant than the ambiguous situations one must pass through to get its reward. Christians have eternal hope. We put little importance on this natural life's condition, recognizing that someone who enjoys excellent provision in this world can be low in spirit.

The cause of unhappiness is not a lack of earthly possessions. And getting wealth does not prevent sadness or eliminate the desire for peace of mind. As Christians, we maintain hope in a supernatural existence that is to come. We look for a celestial dwelling where moth and decay do not corrupt and whose architect and Maker is God. We trust in an unchangeable reality based on God's immutable truth, as established in Jesus Christ. If Jesus is not God and did not become a man to reunite us back to Father God, then everything I live for is futile, and the theme of this work is foolishness. "Faith is the substance of things hoped for and the evidence of things not seen" (Hebrews 11:1). To have faith in something and not lead your life accordingly is like jumping off a ten-story building, recognizing the law of gravity exists, and neglecting its consequences. The invisible realm is inevitable, and its existence is indisputable. God has made His presence obvious (Romans 1:20). We must believe He exists for Him to unveil Himself to us (Hebrews 11:6).

First John 5:20 says, "And we know that the Son of God has come, and has given us an understanding, that we may know Him who is true, and we are in him that is true, in his Son Jesus Christ. This is the true God and eternal life."

We can envision the reality of God in diverse ways. We observe with our eyes and understand that God is engaged in His creation through all our senses. He is noticeable. We can appreciate the elegance and the grandeur of God through the analysis and observation of the universe. We understand the "state of affairs" that occurs in the heavenlies as we employ the force and skills given to us in our capacities to discern and execute. Our ability to cherish and display affection to one another is taking part in the very nature of God. God has expressed His presence to humanity, and He became one of us. By offering Himself through His Son, He has supplied us with what is necessary for us to know Him. In Jesus, He has reached out, extending His right hand of fellowship to His creation, and has entrusted us with the very worth of His Son, the office of "sonship" by which we exclaim "Abba Father." He has caused death and hell to give up their dead and commissioned life to flow in the man, Jesus Christ. Through an intimate relationship with the God of the universe, we get the capacity to realize actual truth. Reality is God's perpetual existence affirmed to us in Jesus Christ, the Son, the true God. God has made His presence known most mysteriously, most remarkably, in the most passionate way imaginable. God is love, and Jesus is God's love revealed to mankind.

CHAPTER 2:

CHAOS IN THE COSMOS

Paul Shepherd accurately commented, "How are your attitudes, thoughts, and words affecting the unseen realm that is all around you? How is the unseen realm that is all around you affecting your attitudes, thoughts, and words?"

For the follower of Jesus, the foundational battle of believing in God or following man's reason and logic is in our minds. Our thoughts, how we react, and what we say have a lot to do with determining whether we have wholly surrendered to the lordship of Jesus Christ. If we hold on to an area of our life based on our ability to reason out why we still have the right to self-govern that section of our life, we claim ownership of it. In doing so, we suggest that we have not surrendered our will to Lord Jesus. Establishing reason above faith is to say that our intelligence is equal to or greater than the One who sustains our every breath. A mistake the author of the original rebellion against the King of kings made.

"And when Jesus had cried out with a loud voice, He said, 'Father, into Your hands, I commit My spirit'" (Luke 23:46). After saying this, He breathed His last. When Jesus made this statement, He accomplished His mission of defeating the hold hell had on humanity once and for all. He then took His rightful place, seated on the throne on high.

Jesus could have made this comment at the start of His public ministry. From the beginning, Jesus committed everything He ever did into the Father's hand. Jesus led a life of obedience, never reasoning His way out of His circumstances. He devoted His thoughts, actions, and words to the Father by confronting life's obstacles with the truth of God's Word, not once applying the principles of darkness in His life. He never attempted to live out His humanity based on the logic of this world.

After committing His life to the Father, He breathed His last. Young's literal translation states, "He breathed forth the spirit."

When we proclaim the end of our life as we know it, by accepting Jesus Christ as Lord, from that point on, all we say or think should express the Spirit of God who lives in us. We should proclaim this spirit breathed life for all to see, "I commit my spirit to Jesus Christ, no longer living for myself, committing all into the Father's hands."

When we come to the Lord Jesus Christ and undergo the reborn experience, we offer our lives to God, creating a new basis for living. We should never again take a breath in this life based on the principles of this world. We have breathed our last breath based on the old sinful human nature; from that point on, every breath we take should be in the newness of life because we are now with Christ seated in the heavenly realm. The breath that gives life to our words should flow from that throne. We should commit our actions, our thoughts, and our comments to the Lord Jesus Christ.

War in the Heavenliness

Scripture is clear that there is a spiritual war going on, and Christians have an archenemy. This enemy has declared war on humankind, specifically those who commit their lives to Jesus Christ as Lord.

Lucifer (Satan's name before sinning), the most beautiful and gifted divine being God created, yielded to pride and rebelled against God. Cast out of heaven, he deceived some angels. These angels gave up their rightful place in the heavenly realm by following him. Satan's marauders are rebellious angels, a host of evil, divine beings, and spirit beings called demons.

Anything we learn about Satan and his hosts of hell should originate in the Word of God. We should learn everything the Bible says about the "evil one" to understand his ways. We should never desire knowledge about Satan from any source other than the Word of God, as this would be like selecting a gourmet meal behind a restaurant by looking in its trash receptacle. Of course, the wealth of documentation written about the subject of spiritual warfare is a valuable resource from which to draw on. However, God's Word must be the foundation for this information. I am referring to leaning on experiences or methods while dealing with darkness. Truth not, the experience should always be our plumbline. Christians should not consult horror movies, ouija boards, tarot cards, seances, or mediums. Books or websites riddled with lies and deceptions also can lead you astray. Satan will always try to deter you from learning that he is and how he operates so that we might remain ineffective in our assault against him. We must be careful to know about Satan based on the truth of God's Word so we do not give the enemy an entryway in our lives. The Holy Spirit must author the revelation about Satan. As we know more about Satan, we must clarify the acceptability of anything we learn from God's Word.

Origin of His Fall

Even though God says that we are never to elevate ourselves, Lucifer exalted himself (Matthew 23:12). Only God has the authority to promote a person (Luke 14:11). Lucifer rebelled against this authority. He degraded himself by decaying the perfection of his being. In Isaiah 14:12, God states "how" twice, referencing Lucifer's choice to rebel against His authority, enabling pride to come into existence. Even though God knew the power of choice brings an individual, Lucifer's decision had to amaze Him. Lucifer was an incredibly divine being. Perfect in every way. God asks, "'How,' oh shining one, son of the dawn, 'how' could you leave all that I have for you and accept the deception that pride and rebellion offer?" It breaks God's heart when we choose to rebel against His authority and exalt ourselves above the throne of God by giving in to pride.

The Fall of Lucifer

In Isaiah 14:12-15, we read how the shining one violated God's authority:

> How you are fallen from heaven, O Lucifer, son of the morning! How you are cut down to the ground, you, who weakened the nations!
>
> For you have said in your heart: "I will ascend into heaven, I will exalt my throne above the stars of God, and I will also sit on the mount of the congregation on the farthest sides of the north;
>
> I will ascend above the heights of the clouds; I will be like the Most High."
>
> Yet you shall be brought down to Sheol, to the lowest depths of the Pit.

The Scriptures give an explicit declaration as to Lucifer's fall from grace (1 Timothy 3:6). His stature and position in God puffed him up. By wanting to move up in rank and elevate himself, he became proud. Lucifer was the crown jewel (cherub) of God's created divine beings, covering all the hosts of heaven. He was the holiest (set apart one) of all that God had made. Yet Lucifer had free will. It requires a free will to bring God the glory from the intimate relationship He desires to have with His created beings, both divine and terrestrial. God, who is all-knowing, was aware of the potential that free will would have. He knew the potential danger the ability to choose without the benefit of complete knowledge could produce. The creation of free moral agents with the ability to choose was more important to God than eliminating the possibility of evil ever coming into existence. In the beginning, evil did not exist. The Bible tells us in Genesis that everything God made was good. Sin is not something God created. It was never a part of His perfect will for creation and is still not a part of His will for us. Sin is not acceptable. Evil came into existence and still exists to this day based on wrong choices. To the degree that God's free moral agents choose incorrectly is the degree that evil exists in their lives. It can only live in those who choose contrary to God's will for their lives. Bad things can happen to you even if you abstain from choosing incorrectly. People all around us are making bad choices. These wrong choices enable evil to exist in the world. Other people's preferences can affect your life. However, evil doesn't have to live in your personal life.

Watchman Nee states, "To violate authority is a principle of Satan."

Rebellion against the authority of God is a principle of Satan. When we contradict God, we might fight directly against Him. We must maintain total dependence on God so we remain covered by the hem of His garment. Because God cannot ignore sin and must be just in everything He does, we must qualify our conduct with the gospel of truth and stand firm by faith in hope clothed with heavenly provision. God will always turn the evil intended for us into good, but we still could suffer unintended consequences if we disobey the Lord, preventing His covering from protecting our lives. The proximity of our lives, where we dwell, should inhabit the presence from on high.

Submission to the authority of God should be our guiding light. The recognition of good and evil should not direct us. The ability to distinguish between good and evil resulted from man's fall; we associate it with the curse, and it should not govern our lives. For to know good and evil is not evidence of obedience to God's will. Every divine being in the unseen realm knows good from evil. Satan tries to get us to rebel against authority any way he can. It doesn't matter if our discernment is accurate. We should never yield to Satan's nature and rebel. If spiritual leaders over us error, we should not judge or condemn them. Instead, in compliance with their delegated authority over us, we should uphold them through prayer. Our knowledge of the good or evil in their lives does not give us the right to rebel by not submitting to their authority. One reason for this is it's God's authority, not His power, that overcomes darkness. God's sovereignty over His created beings, both divine and terrestrial, operates under the principle of submission. God's authority is what

Satan violated. Surrender to God's authority breaks the influence of hell in our lives. Satan rules in this world over the lives of those who choose to follow his example and rebel against God's authority. When we exalt our will above the will of God in our life, we are applying the very principle that Satan used when he attempted to upgrade himself.

Satan doesn't rule this physical world. God's power created everything that exists in our physical reality, and His power sustains it. It (His power) upholds all of creation. In Genesis, we read God breathed forth, and behold, the material universe came into existence. His breath sustains everything that exists. If God were to cease to support this creation, it would no longer exist. God's creative work exists because He spoke it into existence. All the designs of this physical domain live in the mind of God. He created something out of nothing merely by willing it than speaking it into existence.

Watchman Nee said, "The concept of delegated authority works with the principle of submission." It fills the road to authority with milestones marked with submission.

In Luke 7:6-9, we find the centurion's story who approached Jesus and asked Him to heal His son. As Jesus responded to this request, the centurion said that being a man in authority under authority, Jesus just needed to speak under the rulership of God the Father for his (the centurion's) son to experience healing. Jesus' response to this statement is hugely significant. He found no greater understanding of the principle of authority in all of Israel. God's sovereignty in our lives gives us the legal power to stand against the enemy. It is vital to realize who we are in Christ to learn what authority we have in Him. His passion is supreme. If we walk in obedience to Him, we can defeat hell's attempts to destroy us. Submission to God and His control frees us from demonic influence.

Ezekiel 28:13-17 (God's holiness violated):

> You were in Eden, the garden of God; every precious stone was your covering: The sardius, topaz, and diamond, beryl, onyx, and jasper, sapphire, turquoise, and emerald with gold. The workmanship of your timbrels and pipes was prepared for you on the day you were created.

> You were the anointed cherub who covers; I established you; you were on the holy mountain of God; you walked back and forth amid fiery stones.

> You were perfect in your ways from the day you were created, till iniquity was found in you. [*originator of the sinful nature*].

> By the abundance of your trading, you became filled with violence within, and you sinned; therefore, I cast you as a profane thing out of the mountain of God; and I destroyed you, O covering cherub from the midst of the fiery stones.

23

Your heart was lifted up because of your beauty; you

corrupted your wisdom for the sake of your splendor;

I cast you to the ground; I laid you before kings that

they might gaze at you.

Lucifer was the original worship leader created to orchestrate the choir of heaven. The original design of music was to bring glory to the King of kings. Music influences the minds of humankind. Spiritual oneness before the throne of God flows through wholesome music. Satan has perverted the use of music. We see his influence everywhere in the music world. He uses it to captivate and manipulate the sinful desires of man. Lucifer was perfect in every way; there was not one thing that was sub-par in his entire being. It is simply amazing to imagine a being created perfect in every way. It is even harder to imagine having no propensity to sin, nor lack or need of any kind, given the fallen state of creation in the 21st century. However, this was Lucifer's reality when iniquity "was found" in him. Every time we choose to rebel and sin, we do the same thing that he did. We deny God's rightful place in our life, enabling iniquity to operate in us. We defile ourselves by yielding to the sinful nature within us as the forces of darkness attempt to expound on this evil bent and cause us to sin.

Satan Thrown Out of Heaven

And war broke out in heaven: Michael and his angels

fought with the dragon, and the dragon and his an-

gels fought, but they did not prevail, nor was a place

found for them in heaven any longer. So the great dragon was cast out, that serpent of old, called the Devil and Satan, who deceives the whole world; he was cast to the earth, and his angels were cast out with him.

Revelation 12:7-9

When Jesus gave up His spirit on the cross, then rose from the dead, war broke out in heaven. While hanging on the cross, Jesus made the statement, "It is finished." These words marked the end of death's reign over humankind, and it marked the beginning of the heavenly man's rule, Jesus Christ, as well as God's re-established authority over humanity. It was the beginning of a whole new reality in the spirit world. As we know it today, spiritual warfare began the day that Jesus represented a public spectacle of hell by triumphing over it in the cross.

Lucifer, Michael, and Gabriel were angels of the highest order, designed to rule heaven's hosts. These angelic beings were princes designed to reign before the throne of God. We know from Scripture a divine battle raged after the resurrection of Jesus, and they threw an orchestra of angels out of heaven with Satan down to earth. Even though these angels choose to follow his baseless untruths, their conduct must have suggested they would entertain his evil desires. Something caused them to go astray. I could see the hosts of heaven debating and discussing all that had occurred the instant Jesus conquered death. They must have struggled amongst themselves as they tried to convince each other to stand with God or follow Sa-

25

tan. There is no record of the angelic rebellion in heaven and the conduct the angels portray that culminates in them following Satan. Still, their choices had to have made them prime candidates for his deceptive ways. This principle still holds today. If hell can see based on our preferences, our lives might weaken, and our wills can falter by attacking us in specific areas, then torment focuses on that area. He (Satan) will use whatever instrument he can get his hands on to ensnare us (Hebrews 12:1).

The war in the heavenly realm took on a whole new meaning after the crucifixion of Jesus. God threw Satan out of heaven for good. Even though Jesus was in the celestial scene when they escorted Lucifer from heaven for good (Luke 10:18), Satan had to deal with his like kind. The mighty angel Gabriel fought the dragon (Satan), as did Michael, an archangel. A common belief today is that God stands for good and Satan stands for evil. That Satan is the opposite, equal to God. Because Satan is much less powerful than God, this thought could not be further from the truth. Infinite God is all-knowing, everywhere present, and all-powerful. He is consciously aware of everything that ever was, ever will be, and everything that is as if it were today. A self-existent being needs nothing or nobody to sustain His existence. That's why when speaking to Moses, He said, "Tell them I am sent you." The ultimate reality is God. He has always been, and He always will be. "I am that I am." Lucifer (now Satan) exists because God sustains his life. Were God to choose for him to cease to exist, he would be no longer. However, everything that God does is eternal.

With His celestial task here on earth accomplished, here comes the Lord Jesus Christ, walking right up into the heaven of heavens to claim His rightful place at the right hand of the Father. From His glorious vantage point on the throne, Jesus witnesses Lucifer being thrown out of the heavenly divine realm for good; how Lucifer must have felt on that fateful day when God's eternal plan for humanity became apparent to him. He must have thought highly of his abilities, as he had just caused sinful men to crucify the Lord. Having tricked humankind into killing the Son of God through his deceptive devices, he thought his diabolical scheme had accomplished something significant. It did. Only it didn't accomplish what he intended to achieve, for Satan was to enter heaven for the last time and see Jesus seated next to the Father with the hosts of heaven waiting to throw him out of heaven forever. Lucifer's taste of his exalted self was bitter. His (Satan) significant accomplishment was his ultimate demise. Jesus destroyed hell's hold on our lives by being obedient and submitting to the Father. The Lord's submission to the will of the Father beat Satan's legal claim as the accuser of the brethren. Our acquiescence to Jesus eliminates Satan's access to our lives. Obedience and submission to Him (Jesus) destroy darkness. With hell's handle forever broken, we can now live lives free from the death grip of sin.

Satan's rule of rage and terror against humanity comes from a kingdom in exile. His government is through self-deception. His throne is in the second heaven, the atmosphere above the earth. He knows his destiny cannot enter the divine realm again. He knows the man will one day look upon him and ponder how this fallen being could have caused the world to tremble. Even though many people today do not acknowledge Jesus Christ as Lord, most of humanity will come to saving knowledge of Him in this life. Satan is furiously trying to drag as many people to hell with him as he can. But because his influence only stretched across a small percentage of the angelic kingdom (Revelation 12:4), I believe that only a tiny remnant of human beings will choose to deny the lordship of Jesus before their life here on planet earth is over. God's realm of influence is far superior to Satan's, and before the end of creation, God's power will manifest in a great harvest of human souls.

His (Satan) attempt to exalt himself through pride started the rebellion that caused his demise. Pride and rebellion are two of the deadliest sins known to man. Their origin was the root cause of Lucifer's demise. Two of the most significant areas of attack against the church today are pride and rebellion. When God exalts us through His gifting, we should give Him the glory for it. Otherwise, God cannot bless us. If we do not learn how to walk before God, then we limit (Psalm 78:41) His blessing in our lives because He cannot do anything that is not intelligent. If exalting us causes us harm, then He cannot do it. We need to understand how to accept God's blessing and walk before Him in submission and holiness. God has established what is good living and what He does not receive. We are to live humbly before God, being transparent in all we do.

Of the seven deadly sins, pride is king. Pridefulness is like raising a smokescreen to prevent someone from seeing clearly and is a vain attempt at preventing others from seeing us for who we are. It wraps us up in a fog and causes rude and disrespectful behavior. God sets Himself against high-mindedness. Of all the sins that exist, God directly opposes pride. He takes a military stance against it. If pride creeps up in a Christian's life, then God will resist that area in their life. To have God opposing us because we are proud sets us up for attacks of darkness. Pride is thinking that we can safely dwell on the dangerous ground that makes Satan our neighbor. A proud lifestyle removes the fence that separates our safe territory, leaving it full of holes. That's why destruction results from pride. God either abandons that area of our life, or He must oppose it. In either case, we open ourselves up to attack. We are to break up the fallow ground in our lives and remove anything that can let Satan live close.

When someone thinks he is something that he is not, he strays and deceives himself. Feeling important based on an unrealistic sense of self-worth is a risky business. The invention of a cleverly imagined plan of conduct based on a desire to be different may seem innocent enough. However, it can be a spirit of pride. The nature of any evil spirit tries to keep you from knowing it is lying to you. If a spirit of pride is operating in or around you, it will make you think you are more important than others. It will twist the truth to obscure your perception of yourself, preventing you from seeing clearly. However, others usually can see through this charade. Pride calls forth ill-conceived emotions that combat that which is essential to the common good of all, wanting to cause discord. Many serious misfortunes have occurred by not recognizing the influence of evil spirits on our relationships with others.

Anyone who sets themselves above and against others is operating in pride. But to the humble, God gives grace. He gives us the proper amount of skill sufficient for our needs. Before the rise of Christianity, humility did not have the virtue attached to it that the life of Jesus portrayed. It developed a new meaning with the birth of the church. It was honorable to be humble, as the cross of Christ defines it. Highly esteemed humbleness means walking in absolute dependence on God. God wants us to live in His strength. Through modest living, we are to submit to each other in humility. In doing so, we maintain favor with God and man. Humility is the strength of the church. The church is a living organism blessed by God with many parts knit together designed for the Master's task. Lucifer fell because he let his great blessings go to his head. We should understand that all we have, God gives us. He authors all the good in us, leaving us no room to boast. All that we have and all that we are is from Him and for Him. We have these treasures in earthen vessels, a reminder of our humble state as we receive the great blessings from God. So we should never forget that it is God who deserves our praises. We should never attain a position where we cannot associate with individuals who exist in meager surroundings. God's heart is not prideful. It does not exalt itself. He associates with sinners, beggars, the sick, the lowly, and those esteemed as lower-class citizens. He does not wish us to become so sophisticated that we think it is wise to distance ourselves from those less fortunate. We should always recognize that we are all cast from the same mold. We are all in earthen vessels and should agree that we are all chips off the old block (Isaiah 51:1). Natural intelligence requires lowliness. Without it, we can fall into the same snare that caused the Devil to fall.

Christians should never need that anyone should defend them. Instead, they should know that keeping every area of their life open to the gospel of light prevents darkness from penetration. Hell can only live in darkness. Obediently exposing the locations we fail in keeps hell from triumphing over our lives. God's holy presence requires humility and obedience, as these two traits are not feelings or actions but a way of life. Humility, submission, and obedience are the foundational characters of godliness. The opposite of these virtues is identification with the evil's essence that caused Satan to commit the original sin. Sin originated in heaven, not with man. As the first of God's created beings to choose to sin, he (Satan) has been an advocate of sin since its inception. He doesn't care if we sin in ignorance or intentionally, so long as we sin. That's why it is vital to identify sin in our lives and appropriate the blood of Jesus.

Satan grasps at any area he can. Sin will always open up an entryway to our lives. Corruption, known or unknown, enables him access. If we are sinning in an area of our lives and don't think it is wrong, it still opens the door for darkness to live in our lives. God's permissible will is not a place where we can sin and think that His grace covers us from evil. To sin is a failure to develop a proper understanding of the truth. The lies of hell live in darkness. We need a lack of reality for darkness to exist. Demons and evil spirits came into existence because they associated with Satan's dreadful lies.

The unpleasant activity of evil spirits feeds on innocent people who lack knowledge. Christians who have no intention of great evil can do what they do not want to do. It is possible to make harmful decisions, even though you know what is right. As unreasonable as it may seem, you could unexpectedly end up acting contrary to your best interest. Conduct based on flawed principles could get you in trouble. Without understanding the destructive forces at work against us, we can fall prey to some character weakness engaged through natural vices. Natural vices can cause you to choose incorrectly, but making a habit of bad choices could attract wicked spirits' attention.

These evil spirits can occupy many areas identified as emotional disorders. There are spirits of pride, sloth, greed, envy, anger, lust, and gluttony, to name a few. Vile spirits characterized by vicious bents of iniquity want you to think your shameful conduct was your fault when they influenced your actions. They feed on our propensity for evil and attempt to establish themselves in our lives through patterns of habit. A spirit of lust, for instance, can take advantage of our moral misconceptions and gain a foothold into our lives, causing us to act on its evil suggestions. An individual who spends large amounts of time in idle living could become prey to a sloth spirit. A spirit of depression could settle in. Depressed individuals can wind up thinking they are serving no useful purpose in life. They believe they have no excuse for existing. A spirit of death could then suggest committing suicide. After listening to these lies, you might feel so bad you could oppose someone trying to help you. A spirit of jealously might try to keep you from seeing their (your friends) actual intent and convince you they think they are better than you and will look down on you for what you did. If it (the evil spirit) succeeds, this could prevent you from embracing your actual identity. You could rebel against those you are to cooperate with over a simple argument.

Unity in the spirit is a major goal of the Christian life. If you struggle with pride, kindness is a source of strength. A submissive nature promotes modest living. And humility is an inward quality based on a renewed confidence. It is the ability to submit to God while holding up when it's a struggle to keep going and implies the meekness acceptable before God and man. It is that which is central to our existence.

We draw strength from fellow Christians whose faith can impart the fulfillment of the will of God in our lives. We must stand against attempts to make malicious or knowingly false statements about somebody. Errors in our opinions set us up for an attack from hell and eventually cause us to stumble. Loss and suffering are part of life. But events resulting in significant loss and misfortune sometimes result when you do not take proper stances against the dark forces at work against us.

The power that makes us successful belongs to God. It's His property and proceeds from His being. The divine light that sets us apart is a gift. Always maintain a posture of dependency on Father God. That we need Him keeps Him at the center of our lives. He should sit on the throne of our lives. Our wills should be in subjection to His will. He gives us excess per His fullness and sets our sights way beyond what we could ever accomplish on our own. Like in the book of Judges chapter 7, we are all glorious lights of God's glory waiting to manifest. We are to live our lives in the manner set out by the Holy Scriptures so people can see God's glory through living epistles. Brokenness and humility are part of the character of Christ. God's light shines forth through brokenness. We cannot show the true greatness of the glory of God in our lives without it. God will not despise a broken and contrite heart. Satan authored the selfish ambition called self-interest. God alone exalts. We should always consider how to enlarge the kingdom of God by placing the value on people that God does. If we can see people through God's eyes, then compassion and understanding are immediate responses towards them.

Unlike God's kingdom, the nature of the community of the Devil is altogether void of any truth at all. Those who oppose the gospel stand on the ground paved by darkness; hell is their foundation, and the lie of Satan rules their reasoning. By their choices, they have headed for the same inevitable doom as the angels of hell who rebelled with Satan. However, even though it is always a man who walks away from God, He never leaves us. When we find ourselves outside of the estate of heaven, it takes away our original place of authority. We need to re-establish our proper location, which is right in the middle of God's will for our lives. Unlike the angels who ran away from home unable to return, we can choose to return to the Father when we stumble. Like little children who ran away from home for what seemed to be a good reason, then realizing it was a mistake, we should come running back with arms outstretched into the loving grasp of Father God.

CHAPTER 3:

EVIL IS REAL

Throughout known history, there seems to exist a constant struggle between good and evil. Though people can view this perpetual conflict with varying opinions, one certainty seems unavoidable. We executed many crimes against humanity. The circumstances behind these many atrocities change, but inevitably one concludes it is possible to experience a force in nature that governs conduct detrimental to other individuals. Contrary to society's popular opinion, these are not random acts perpetrated by selfish desire or propensities governed by mere acts of volition. No, I believe the singular cause behind these evils has successfully disguised itself from the beginning. According to Old Testament scholars, Satan (Revelation 12:9) was not a proper name during Old Testament times. As an adjective, it means slanderer or accuser. However, this term appropriately became the name applied to the evil spirit we see engaging Eve as the serpent during the garden of Eden scene. When Adam and Eve sinned, Satan hid his supernatural identity in that serpent to deceive the first couple. Of all the horrendous tragedies executed by Satan, the greatest conspiracy he ever successfully perpetrated on humanity has been the ability to conceal his existence from them. To this day, many Christian communities deny the existence of that evil divine being who first burst on the scene of humanity in the garden of Eden. He is not a figment of our imagination, nor is he merely a personification of evil. Satan, the embodiment of evil, has become the most formidable evil spirit being that exists.

This divine being is the original architect of sin as we know it and has been hostile toward the things of God from the day of his rebellion. His actions have opposed humankind from the first day human beings appeared on the scene. When he caused humankind to sin for the first time, he concealed his true intention and his identity. In fact, to this day, he is still hiding his intents and purposes behind his many disguises. Satan has emerged as the prince of the entire evil spirit realm. As the passageway to hell, he encourages people to defy God. The Devil is always trying to make sin seem pleasurable, knowing full well the consequence of sinning is distasteful, dangerous, and ultimately fatal.

Satan uses thoughts, words, appearance, lust, fear, suspicions, anger, confusion, friends, strangers, family, enemies, physical and spiritual things to achieve his goal for you. However, he is predictable in his attacks against us because his bag of tricks is small. Unfortunately, he doesn't need new tricks because the old ones work so well.

Every communication coming from the Devil is in his native tongue (falsehood). He is the originator of knowing, desiring, deciding, and acting in opposition to God. He is constantly twisting truisms to get Christians to buy into his distorted version of the truth. Using his deception tactics, he tries to dissuade us from believing the Bible to be the inerrant word of God. If we question God's Word, the Devil can attempt to use our inability to adhere to the law to convince us that God's grace is not sufficient payment for our sins. One of his favorite pastimes is to humiliate people when they fail by making legal accusations against them. He is always trying to imprison people through his persuasive methods of cunning and worldly wisdom by continuously creating falsehood. He is the one who causes distrust among brethren, trying to get us to turn on one another.

Through his attempts to imitate God, Satan solicits sin through malicious and crafty deception. Repulsive to God's ways, he is impious, vile, worthless, and inflicts evil whenever he can. He produces hardship and annoyances to bring troublesome times, always trying to cause pain and disappointment. The goal of his unclean method is to tear down the Christian community. However, with God's help, we can overcome him.

Adversary, which means one who opposes another in purpose or act, is one name given to the prince of evil spirits, the inveterate adversary of God and Christ.

1) He incites apostasy from God and to sin,

2) circumvents men by his wiles,

3) controls idol worshippers, and

4) by his demons, he can inflict humans with diseases.

However, upon Christ's return to earth from heaven, the Lord will bind Satan with chains for a thousand years. At the end of the thousand years, he (Satan) will walk the globe in a yet greater power, but his inevitable destiny as the lord of the dead is eternal punishment.

The Greek transliteration for Devil is *diabolos*. It comes from two roots. *Dia*, meaning "the ground or reason by which something is or is not done," and *ballo*, "to throw or let go of a thing without caring where it falls; to give over to one's care, uncertain about the result."

Satan (also called the Devil) is one of the primary causes behind the evil we do and the leading force preventing us from doing the good we want. He exists in our lives only if we allow him to establish legal ground. If he can gain this ground, he throws us around, not caring what happens to us. When we give him environments to work with, we can never be sure of the outcome.

Satan purposely attempts to steal anything he can from us (John 10:10). The word for stealing in Greek is *kleptes*. Its root means "to commit a theft; to take away by stealing." It is where we get our word *klepto*, which means "an irrational urge to steal void of an economic motive." Though Satan steals because of an uncontrollable urge, he steals skillfully; he takes a little at a time. If allowed legal access, he will not hesitate to enter our domain, kill, steal, and destroy anything that impedes his diabolical purpose for us. If he gains our confidence, it is always to his advantage. He wants to make us living sacrifices, becoming victims of his ways. He wants to tear down anything that God has established in us. In sharp contrast, the eternal sufficiency of Christ sustains all of humanity by the word of His power (Hebrews 1:3).

He (Satan) can hear what we say and try to influence our thoughts with malicious purposes. Learn to know if and where he affects you

38

so you can resist his worthless ways. He is constantly devising evil plans against us, attempting to take us captive by his intentions. Any area of our life he controls is a place he can rule (like a king or judge). If we grant him legal rights, he will place a seat of power to rule over a specific area of our life, like his legal right to rule as the prince (for a particular time) of the power of the air (the lower, denser atmosphere) (Ephesians 2:2), where his throne is. He also has fallen divine beings of darkness and demons at his disposal to resist us. They are subject to his authority, and even though they have rebellious natures, they share the same common goal of destroying humanity.

Satan will always question authority (Matthew 4:6). One of his appeals to Jesus in the desert was to defy gravity. The Devil urged presumptuous reliance on God, contrary to the natural laws of His creation, and quoted Scripture to support his view (Psalm 91:11). So the Devil quotes Scripture, misinterprets it, omits a clause, and tries to deceive the Son of God by the Word of God. Not very smart. The Devil thought the promise of deploying the angels would reassure Jesus. They would be a spiritual parachute for Christ. God never promises to protect us if we act thoughtlessly. His mercy, grace, and love cover a multitude of sins. However, we tread on dangerous ground if we think we can carry His protection around with us like our own personal safety net.

Satan Was an Anointed Cherub

Scripture does not explicitly tell us that Lucifer was an archangel, but it says he had rank and authority (Ezekiel 28:14). Michael, an archangel, did not verbally assault him directly (Jude 9) during their altercation over the body of Moses. One thing is sure. God favored him as one of His most fabulous creations. As previously alluded to, it's easy to understand that our fallen nature causes us to sin. Still, it seems unbelievable how a perfect, wise divine creation without the propensity to sin fell from heaven.

Satan Has Nothing in Me

The statement Jesus made about Satan having nothing in Him is one of the most potent truths ever conveyed to humanity (John 14:30). Jesus withstood evil, not entertaining the slightest of sinful thoughts. A source of strength for us is the fact that in Jesus, evil never existed. Contrary to what some false religions maintain, the evil one exists. Jesus knew Satan to be a real being (John 8:44). But Satan's realities can only live under certain conditions. The spiritual darkness in a person can only exist if a person lets it continue. Evil exists; this is a fact. But evil does not have to live in your individual life. Jesus did not deny Satan's rule of this world's system; He restrained his (Satan) authority over His own life. If you live a life of reverence, taking every thought captive to obedience in Christ Jesus, acknowledge and confess any sin that might trip you up; then, there is no secrecy in you. If there is no obscurity in you, then to you, evil does not exist. Satan rules this world because humankind has yielded to him, giving him authority to rule. As previously mentioned, it is God who governs the physical laws of nature. Therefore, Satan cannot make the earth fall off its axis, nor can he make the sun or the moon change its orbits. His rule is a rule over the bad choices people make. To the degree that he can influence people's will is the degree he rules this world. He controls only the areas of this world that function per his principles. So if we decide to keep him out of our lives, he has nothing in us. If we choose to say (by obedient living) that based on the principle of God's Word, we will resist darkness; then, he cannot exist in any area of our lives. To Jesus, evil did not exist. We must follow this example and prevent Satan from having the right to live in our lives.

The way the church approaches the reality of Satan is lacking. We seem to think that if we focus our attention on him, we might stir up a hornet's nest. If we make declarations and attack darkness, something terrible might happen. Satan might notice us if we speak against him. Then we will be in serious trouble because he might focus his energy on us and come after us. If we leave him alone, maybe we will go unnoticed. After all, aren't Christians supposed to be gentle lovers of God and not violent agents? Aren't Christians to focus on the love of God and the lordship of Jesus, and the evil things of this world will take care of themselves. I am not saying that our focus should be darkness. We are to glorify God with our lives and focus on the leading of His divine Spirit. But when we lead someone to Christ and choose to expand the kingdom of God, whose kingdom do you think we are penetrating? I remember a song with lyrics that said, "I went to the enemy's camp, and I took back what he stole from me." Some of you might have trouble with these lyrics because you might think we should not enter the enemy's camp. I've got news for you. We live right smack dab in the middle of the enemy's camp. And it's his camp that shrinks when we expand God's kingdom by convincing a new believer that Jesus Christ is Lord.

With an offensive posture, we are to stand against darkness in the authority of the Holy Spirit. Satan's acts are for personal purposes perpetrated. Like in the garden, they are apparent in action but secret in intent. Satan restrains and hinders us to prevent us from breaking out of his grasp. We need to wake up and take back any grounds the Devil has stolen. We are at war; the increase of the kingdom of God reduces the kingdom of darkness. We execute violence into the enemy's camp every time we do something for the kingdom of God. If you think you can go unnoticed in this war, you are mistaken. When you become a Christian, a neon light goes on, and your name gets pasted up on the billboard of hell. From that point on, you become a target of torture. No matter whether we fight Satan covertly or overtly, he is warring against us. Satan has deceived the church. He has placed a veil of darkness over our understanding. Christian leaders today seem concerned with overemphasizing Satan and his influence. As if this is a big problem in the church. The church's problem is there is little or no emphasis placed on hell's tactical attacks. As the source of original sin, everything he (Satan) has ever done or ever will do is sin. Lawlessness is the character of all divine evil powers. There is direct opposition between the kingdom of Satan and Christ's kingdom. If you attempt to stand on neutral ground, you will get caught in the crossfire.

Despite the battle going on for the lives of humanity, Satan is under God's rule, and the Holy Spirit restrains demonic activity. If this were not so, Satan would destroy everything and everybody. However, in his iniquity, he continually shows contempt for God and violates God's law. Evil purpose with malice is his every desire; with wickedness as his operating system, he breaches and transgresses everything possible. Because Satan's actions require darkness, secret sinful areas in our lives give him an arena in which to work. He works in private and must function hidden from the light. By shedding light through confession and transparent living, we break his hold on our lives. Light breaks his ability to perform and stops his activity. When Satan's rule over the earth ends, all will see the mystery of lawlessness for what it is. Even though the deceptiveness of corruption is so prevalent in the world today, at the end of time, God will reveal the secret purposes of hell.

Iniquity is an action. Lawlessness is a heart attitude. Sins of iniquity are not as challenging to deal with as is a corrupt heart. Iniquity violates God's holiness; sins of the heart violate God's authority. Christians maintain a positional sinless state in Christ; however, their actions are not faultless, and a rebellious nature opposes God. You violate God's sovereignty by unbelief and rebellion. A contrary, unbelieving person shows he is still king of his own life, a state that keeps us separated from God. Sin breaks a Christian's fellowship with God. But salvation is not something that you fall in and out of based on conduct. A Christian has determined in his spirit that Jesus is Lord. However, holiness is evidence of salvation. A person who establishes a personal relationship with God through faith ceases to live a lifestyle of sin. It is a transformation that occurs based on inward work. Satan cannot condemn a Christian to hell. He can, however, influence a Christian and break his effectiveness and fellowship with Father God.

Satan attempts to get a foot in the door of your life any way he can. If he succeeds, this foothold, if not dealt with, can become a stronghold. A stronghold is a spiritual, mental fortress fortified by evil conduct. However, the real danger lies in uncalculated thoughts or emotions perpetually running adrift, eventually becoming random acts leading to reoccurring sin. Learn to identify the conjectures of hell before sin becomes habitual.

The foundation of any activity that can eventually become a habit originates in our minds. Erroneous thinking can become a secure source of defense for the Devil. If an evil spirit can penetrate our minds and incarcerate our thoughts, it can develop a measure of control over us. Like taking shelter behind the walls of a military fortress, this control gives the Devil a secure place of influence in our thought-life. Trouble comes if you let these sympathetic thoughts continue to penetrate your mind. Left unchecked, they could gain a measure of control over your thinking patterns. If we blow it because we give in to wrong thinking, the Devil is always there to cheer us on.

A demon is always trying to deprive you of your legal rights. One way it does this is by getting you to wrongfully or dishonestly apply these rights. Be wary of anyone not teaching a sound doctrine that causes you to stray from Jesus, as words not founded on Christian ethics with faith and love in operation are not beneficial. Like the inclination to profit from dishonest practices, inappropriate compensation for acts of benevolence when helping others can cause them to lose heart and become discouraged if they think their best interest is not your primary goal. We should help others carry their burden in life; we teach and instruct others through beliefs based on proper moral considerations. It is necessary to always fully know your true identity in Christ Jesus, or your life's pure intentions can erode into failures.

The craving for worldly gain is a pitfall of many evil trials. Situations and circumstances that can cause you to sin come into existence when the desperateness of this temporal desire leads you astray. A passion for money at all costs is costly. Grief and pain consume a person who lets greed penetrate deep into their soul. Every day, a Christian is to live righteously, with feelings of humility and meek living being part of their lifestyle. It is the heart's attitude that determines right or wrong standing with the Lord. Riches are not evil. God does not call us to embrace a spirit of poverty. However, the foundation of our intentions should always be the golden rule. Inattentive to our interests, we should devote ourselves to the well-being of others. As we ponder the outcome of the things we do, we should consider the equity of all. By being a servant to others, we value people with the value God established by paying the price for their sins. Taking care of others allows God to take care of you. We should rest in the confidence that God supports and covers our lives.

The Devil loves it when we use temporal means to provide for our ministries. He seeks to get us to provide for our needs through incorrect means, thus nullifying our effectiveness against him. Many Christians have fallen into the snare of using the gospel for selfish gain.

He also loves it when we perform seemingly divinely inspired miracles with our own proper or necessary skills. Never act on God's behalf unless you get clear direction from the Lord. Likewise, we should never use our God-given abilities to bring attention to ourselves. We might disguise what we do as being from God, but self-effort deprives God of His legal, official rights and privileges and declares our efforts unqualified.

A challenging and disagreeable position in life does not mean that God is not favoring you. Obedience is a conscious act amid challenging circumstances. In our private lives, we are to obey and be subject to God in all things. Self-sufficiency in God's abundance is finding contentment in what you need. It is inward confidence knowing the Lord's provision will supply all your needs. The strength designed to satisfy our soul comes from above. He not only keeps us, but He prevents many dangers contrary to His will for us from affecting us. His abiding presence suffices to support not only our present needs but any future troubles that might come our way as well. As Christians, we do not find fulfillment in our accomplishments because our ultimate destination is with Christ in heavenly places. The fact is, we arrived here with nothing, and only the godly things we accomplish will continue with us when this life is over. Great men of renown from the past have tried to mummify themselves and pack worldly riches for their journey into the afterlife, only to have their wares pilfered by future generations. Nothing goes with us except for the results of our actions.

CHAPTER 4:

TEMPTATION

To the Extent that You Sin, Demons Influence You

Jesus was unlike Old Testament priests (Hebrews 4:15). They had to atone for their sins and those of the communities. The life that Jesus lived was free from any wrongdoing. He did not need to atone for His sin, as there was no sin in Him, not even a hint of latent immorality lingering around for misery to arouse through temptation. Jesus experienced weaknesses like hunger, thirst, and fatigue, which can lead to exploitation if inappropriately surrendered to (John 4:6). Yet, in His humankind, He resisted Satan's most strenuous attempts to thwart Him. Because of this, His empathy for our struggles is genuine.

In this life, Jesus walked in the natural spirit common to fellow man. His human form was like ours, as He was prone to the same propensities that all human beings experience (Mark 3:5, John 11:35, 12:27). As a man, He used only His human attributes to endure the cross path. Using the divine Spirit's completeness, whose capacity to undertake everyday experiences is available to all men, He withstood sin. We can sometimes find reluctance to doing what is right, which makes it difficult not to sin, especially during a tough time. However, not resisting temptation shows the cowardice of heart that contributes to further exploits from the netherworld. It, too, cannot offer God proof that our trust in Him is sufficient, able to prevent us from falling into Satan's pitfalls. All temptation has its limitations. It cannot grow to a point where we cannot bear it unless we let it. There is always a way out (1 Corinthians 10:13). The inclination by hell intended for the ill is potentially a medium for good. By enduring it, we prove God's competence in us to accomplish His will for our hearts. In a judicial sense, the trial itself approves you, as a court proceeding must occur for somebody to receive an acquittal. The case in a court of law confirms the approval. Similarly, when we face temptation, the proof is in the test itself. After walking victoriously through trickery, the crown we receive is not just a crown of royalty but also the pinnacle of a conquering warrior (James 1:12).

Temptation does not come from God as He does nothing evil (James 1:13). His knowledge comes from infinite wisdom, which knows the folly of entertaining evil in any form. You cannot tempt God by sin because He knows the inevitable outcome of every action. Experiencing corruption is the outcome of yielding to temptation; the idea of succumbing to such action does not even enter His mind. By understanding every action's development before it occurs, He will not entertain evil thoughts. God cannot author injustice or give birth to evil because every "perfect" gift comes from the Father above. Sin does not exist in Him, and thus, He cannot give birth to corruption in any form. Evil is entirely foreign to His being and thought process.

If humanity were to see into the spiritual reality of things, they would see that Satan's plan for their lives destroys their souls. Again,

Satan controls the kingdom of men to the extent they choose to take part in his deceptiveness. His rule's deceitful cunning is solely and simply over a yielded human spirit's sinfulness through transitory desire at a spiritual loss. He seeks to make it seem like immediate gratification is okay. He wants to make us subservient to him and not to God.

Sin is always crouching at the door of our minds, attempting to ignite the fallen nature within us. Through temptation, sin entices us, trying to drag our corpses away like a dead weight. When the lure of temptation ignites in us a propensity to sin, our body of death awakens, arousing curiosity like an animal lured away from its den. At which time, it could be too late to retreat to safety. When our thought life engages with a sinful desire, it's like two men hanging from a cliff with hands clasped together as if at the end of their rope. One slip of the wrist, and down you go. Thoughts united with emotion ignite our will and give birth to action. At inception, sin can fully dismantle us. Left unchecked, it grows complete in its function. This function is a life given over to iniquity. Hell always wants to derail us, preventing us from maintaining our union with Christ. Death springs forth in us by uniting our will with our fallen nature like a careless young person free of parental restraint for the first time in their life. Unrestrained and free to act out their destructive desires is how sin matures in an individual's life. So we find that giving birth to evil in our hearts brings spiritual death, and death to our sinful desires brings spiritual life.

Obedience is a learned experience. It is coming to understand discipline through participation. Jesus did not come down from heaven with the knowledge to be obedient in this life. He did not need this knowledge in heaven. For Jesus to learn obedience in His humanity, He had to learn compliance by going through the actual suffering itself (Hebrews 5:8). Jesus needed to experience growth through the natural process because this is an essential part of human development. Because He suffered for our disobedience, His obedience before God broke hell's power over us. We shatter the strength of suffering in our lives by being loyal to the call of God. God's will, expressed in His Word and through the Holy Spirit, equips us with the ability to withstand the temptations of hell. The act of obedience to the Father allows us to resist temptation. Baptism is symbolic of this spiritual lifestyle we live out in the power of God. It serves as a symbol of the spiritual warfare we are in. However, death to self is a conscious choice engaged in practical, everyday living. In Christ, our spiritual death is as actual as being physically dead. Like being rescued from a bottomless pit, we can face temptation without fear because the hope we have in Jesus saves us from past, present, and future evils (2 Corinthians 1:10).

In the desert scene, Jesus successfully suffered the onslaught of the enemy's evil temptations. Like He did throughout His life, He withstood every attempt of hell known to man to overthrow Him. Because He did this in His humanity, He can aid us in our weaknesses (Hebrews 2:18). His ability to help us is as tangible as a parent's ability to assist their child. When distress comes our way, we can come running to Him for aid with arms flailing in the air because we know Jesus will rescue us from a very present evil.

Method of Temptation

Body-soul-spirit/way-truth-life/priest-prophet-king

Human beings possess a body, a soul, and a spirit. The physical body being neutral is the part of us that interacts with this material world and is the vehicle sin travels on if we choose to proceed down the path of perdition. Our soul is where our mind, emotions, and our will live. It is the steering mechanism determining the course of life we choose to travel on. Our spirit is the drive-train that energizes our journey and is the part of us that will live forever.

So like God, we are a tripart being. God is three persons in one: the Father, the Son, and the Holy Spirit. The ministry of Jesus is also tripart; He is the High Priest, the Prophet, and the soon coming King. The incarnate Yahweh provides us with a three-part message as well. He is the way, the truth, and the life. These are a few of the correlations that convey the majesty of God's glorious trinitarian presence and the continuity of His unique creation.

Satan's attack on Eve was threefold. He attacked Eve's body by tempting her with food. He then attacked her soul by enticing her emotionally. Finally, he attacked her spirit with worldly desire. If we forget Jesus is the Bread of Life (John 6:33, 35, 48, 51) and that we are to keep our eyes on Him (Hebrews 12:2) and understand that He gives life to our spirit (John 3:16, 36-5:24), then Satan can come in and try to usurp God's will in our life.

So it should come as no surprise that the enemy's temptation method against us is threefold (1 John 2:16). As he did in the garden to Eve, he attacks our desire for physical pleasure (body), the craving for things we see (soul), and becoming proud of our accomplishments (spirit). He causes us to sin in a variety of ways, but his mode of operation is fundamental.

This three-fold process is the same method Satan used when he tempted Jesus in the wilderness. By misquoting Scripture, he attempted to get Jesus to sin on three different occasions:

He wanted Jesus to command the stones to turn into bread (body).

He wanted Jesus to jump off a cliff and ask angels to keep Him from falling to death (soul).

If He would only bow down and worship him, he offered to make Jesus ruler of the kingdoms of the earth (spirit).

Jesus resisted this tripart onslaught by correctly quoting the Word of God. When Satan attacks, it is always with lies. It is vital to understand the truth of God's Word because Satan will try to distort God's plan for our lives. He makes it seem like God will protect us, even if we don't do what His Word says. When evil approaches, immediately create a stand. We should not listen to any of the enemy's lies. If we do, the outcome is always despairing. God and only God should reign in our hearts. Our service in this life should always be for the Master's cause. Like with Jesus in the desert, accomplishing God's will always bring replenishment to our spirits.

Stay close to the Lord so you can experience the security of abiding under the shadow of the Almighty. We must choose to put on the entire armor of God to withstand the mind strategies and bodily assaults of the slanderer (Romans 5:2). As citizens of heaven, our conduct reflects our belief system. Our ability to change our behavior based on the Scriptures' knowledge allows us to stand against the reproaches of this life. So we are to manage our lives as ambassadors of Christ, correctly handling the state of heaven's affairs. Like athletes in concert together striving for the same goal, we are to walk by faith, believing that He can keep us from falling. Faith is an act of bringing into existence that which is available to us. It requires faith to resist darkness. Grace is the unique privilege of God's provision made accessible by faith. Hope is the level ground on which we are to stand to access this superior position before God. Unless we stand in grace with full assurance of God's provision made available by faith to resist darkness, then Satan can move in to influence us to act contrary to God's will.

Visual yearning manifests by contemplating desire in the mind. If we leave our soul unprotected and we lust with our eyes or through our thoughts, we usually sin with our bodies. After yielding our souls to a sinful vice and act out through our bodies, the enemy can directly attack our spirits. Lust is not only sensual; it can also be a longing for other illicit things. It is a desire that lives in the flesh. Our flesh is separate from our physical bodies. Our bodies being neutral are not sinful. You can use your body for good or evil. When contemplated sin ignites our emotions, it spawns desire in our carnal, sinful flesh. This improper desire is enmity with God. For example, inappropriate pride is trusting in the earthly things we get through our resources and can lead to empty boasting. This kind of thinking is like a homeless person who accumulates belongings through deception. Though steeped in poverty, he desires attention and wants to get people to exalt their opinion of him. This temporal mindset is evidence that a person does not understand divine treasures.

God, whose motive is always mercy, expects us to respond appropriately to His call. We are to function in the service of God like the Old Testament life of a priest who devoted all his physical liberties to the work of God. Our body, being the outward instrument of our will, is to be active in doing good. This action results from rational living based on the highest kind of reason. This lifestyle is well-pleasing to the Father. The sum of the law is a pattern of this type of godly residence. Through a change in our inner being's essential qualities, we develop a lifestyle that reflects the proper form of a child of God. Intelligent choices based on moral purity result in this type of living. We are not to fashion ourselves to the allurements of this life. The distinctive character of these fleeting allurements prevents us from experiencing the eternal liberties in Christ.

By requiring our body to yield to our will, it becomes subject to our choices. Our choices should never be subject to our bodies to live out our potential evil desire. By not allowing our bodies to take part in this world's sinful activities (Romans 12:1), our minds can experience the renewing that comes through the washing of the Word of God (Romans 12:2). This cleansing presence of God reveals His will for our entire being. The basis of proper alignment is good principled Christian living.

Good Christian living is not perfection but obedience. By becoming familiar with how Satan works, we can apply the gospel's principles to his attacks. To err is human, to admit it is divine. It is crucial to acknowledge when we fail, confess it, and shed light on the area of darkness in our lives. By humbling ourselves before God and each other, we can learn how walking in the Spirit can change our lives—being Christian enables us to live according to godly principles and apply them through practical living. Christianity is not mystical. Through everyday living, we can experience the fullness of God in our lives.

After He began His public ministry, the first recorded words of Jesus Christ were "It is written." These words should be the defense of every child of God. From the beginning of our journey with God, God's written Word should be our foundation for living, the gauge for the decisions we make. As truth in a tangible form, it should help achieve the victorious life availed to us by Father God, the sustainer of life.

As previously alluded to, when we become Christian, a billboard lights up in the halls of hell. Satan notes our conversion and sends his minions to trip us up in ways specific to us. When temptation comes, its clear intent is to defeat us at the attack's particular time. Satan's minions base the plan for our lives on the knowledge they have of our generational lineage and us. God intends for us to withstand temptation, thus becoming more vigorous. In doing so, we can mature into more usefulness in God's economy.

It is important to remember that the tempter does not stop questioning who we are in Christ; he questions our Christian walk's genuineness. If he can get us to doubt our credibility, he can cause us to self-examine ourselves. We must maintain confidence in our legitimacy based on who we are in Christ in every situation.

The Temptation of Jesus

Like Jesus in the wilderness, the ability to not eat for days is another valuable source for developing strength to resist hell. That's because not eating raises our spiritual antennas. It tunes our spirit to the frequencies of heaven. This communing with God is a valuable tool because God, who is the author of our authentic life, provides us with the heavenly nourishment needed to resist hell.

During the temptation of Jesus, I've often wondered if Satan could instantly transport Jesus to various places. The Bible seems to move from each scene rapidly. Herod's temple, the pinnacle where Jesus' second temptation occurred, stood 450 feet above the Kidron Valley and represented holy highness. A spiritual exaltation. Satan offers us loftiness to make us quiver with excitement and anticipation. But if we yield to him, the empty promise of spiritual exaltation becomes nothing more than a downward spiral into utter ruin. Satan continually makes it seem like he has more to offer us than he does. He controls nothing but that which is illegitimate. His control over this world's kingdoms and the glory that comes with it is through his deception.

Although the temptation of Jesus in the desert was initially a mental attack, they were also physical. The Devil was physically tempting Jesus to misuse His thought processes. Most physical attractions start as an attack on the mind. If we yield to hell's suggestions, our imaginations can become the Devil's playground. He will try to entice us with glorious visions and lure us into desiring that which belongs only to God. We should never choose to have control over such things, as only the Lord Himself should govern.

CHAPTER 5:

TACTICAL STRATEGY

The Bible states angels of differing degrees and various job descriptions intervene on our behalf, helping to bring about God's will (Exodus 23:20). They render help in specific ways. In Acts (12:5a, 7, 8), the corrections officer guarding the prisoners did not realize or hear the angels assisting Peter when they (the angels) helped him escape from prison, yet they were there. Angels will assist us physically and spiritually. By nudging us in the right direction, they divert our attention away from darkness and toward God. They help us rise when we are down and remove bondage chains from our lives by shedding light on our circumstances. During the Apostle Peter's day, common Jewish belief was that every person had a "guardian angel." This concept is an area of debate in the modern church. One thing seems clear, angels communicate and interact in the lives of human beings.

God provides safety in a variety of ways if we abide close to Him. Walking according to His ways affords us His complete protection. His mercy provides security as personified by abiding under the shadow of His wings (Psalm 91:1-4), stretching across us as we stay in the secret place through trust. Scripture tells us that sin separates us from God. If we are living in sin, we cannot adhere closely to the Almighty. Unlike being able to take a blanket with you wherever you go, to receive the entire covering of God, we must remain close to Him. We cannot dwell in the secret place unless our hands are clean and our hearts are pure (Psalm 24:3-4). This purity and cleansing result from faith in the death, burial, and resurrection of Jesus Christ as payment for our trespasses.

We are to gird ourselves with this faith to avoid being led astray. Through preparation, we protect our walk, preventing injury. Our lives can become vulnerable to attack unless we maintain proper camouflage. We are to conceal ourselves with the clothing of the Lord (Isaiah 61:10). When God frees us from bondage, we receive clear direction for our lives. He thoroughly prepares us for the tasks ahead. Peter's deliverance was not an anxious self-attempt to free himself from prison. It was God calmly equipping him for freedom and, during dark circumstances, delivering him ultimately and calmly from hell's intent for his life.

Satan would love to keep a continuous hold in our lives. He is always hovering over us, trying to keep us from getting free from his grasp. Hell intends to prevent us from seeing into the spiritual realm and distinguishing the voice of the Lord; however, Satan is not as clever as he thinks he is with the things of God. Though his attacks take on many forms, Satan's method is predictable, and his attack plan is detectable. As creatures of habit, these attacks target our specific weaknesses. Once we realize this, we can counterattack. We need to develop a spiritual radar when dealing with his method of madness to subdue his attacks before they cause us harm.

Satan has many names associated with the myriad of ways in which he attacks. He takes on various forms against the Christian and the Christian Church. Of the many titles attributed to Satan, two primarily descriptive titles are adversary and slanderer. Through his modus operandi, he causes adversity and accuses us. Unconcerned with unbelievers because his deception is already at work in them, unless, of course, he senses the Holy Spirit getting close to revealing Himself to them, his strategies attempt to penetrate Christians' lives. In doing so, he prevents them from obtaining their inheritance here on planet earth. A primary intention is to confuse, misuse, and abuse us in any way he can. He wants to prevent us from understanding our true identity in Christ Jesus, knowing that we will effectively invade his kingdom if we grasp the truth of our authority. He knows he can do very little regarding the Christian's ultimate resting place in the eternal realm. Fellowship with God in eternity is the timeless destination of all the followers of Jesus and is not subject to his temporal rule. However, here on earth, our arch-enemy will take all the territory you allow him to take. Demonization refers to the influence or control that a demon or evil spirit has over a person. This influence will conflict with God's will for our spiritual, physical, mental, emotional, and social lives. We must resist.

Satan's deceptive knowledge and experiences make him a cunning adversary. He can watch us from birth, and as mentioned, he also has developed information regarding our weaknesses and faults by observing our ancestry. Because he questioned God, he constantly challenges us. Lying is his native tongue; he tries to change the truth God wants to communicate to us and pervert God's intent for us. Never forget that we are to learn about the evil one through God's Word, not by conversing with darkness. Because of Satan's deceptive ability, Eve should not have responded when he questioned her. She should have relied on what she knew to be true. When he confronts us, we shouldn't defend ourselves using logic; instead, we should rely on Scripture's truth. God told Eve not to eat from the tree, which was in the "midst of the garden." He said nothing about not touching it. We should never take the Word of God out of context. In doing so, we can inappropriately apply it to life's circumstances. It is essential to know what the Bible says to prevent deception (2 Timothy 2:15). We should become so familiar with the Word of God that it permeates our entire being. The truth of God's Word is the foundation of life. Its validity has the authority to stop the lies of the Devil (Psalm 119:11).

When Lucifer sinned, he tasted the horror of separation from God. Because of his disobedience, he became familiar with the empty and void knowledge that good and evil creates; tasting this bitter consequence, he wanted Eve to experience the same spiritual death he had. He could taunt Eve with a lie because she was not familiar with the concept of separation from God. Because Eve did not know spiritual death existed, she could not have understood the consequence of eating the forbidden fruit. The dread of divine separation from God was something she could not comprehend. We should never govern our lives based on the principle of the power of good and evil. By maintaining our relationship through obedience and submission to authority, we can avoid the pain of broken fellowship with God. Through observation, Eve needed to take charge of the attack from the serpent by factoring Adam into the equation. Submission to God's delegated authority is key to maintaining the protection that Scripture promises. Obedience, not worldly wisdom, should be the motivating factor that governs our lives. This world's logic can lead us astray if we are not familiar with the eternal *truth* of God's Word.

Never proposing to be clever or cunning enough in our attempts to put off hidden things, we are to use the Scriptures, not carnal wisdom, to stop the darkness. We are to speak out against the secret deeds of evil, trying to displace and remove them. We are to live transparent lives in harmony with God's Word to prevent sin from controlling us by understanding Jesus has cleared us from any charge hell brings against us. To error in our understanding of the Scriptures causes corruption.

The World in Which We Live

Things are not always what they seem. Godless logic is like having a meal prepared for a king that merely needed salt to be complete, then sprinkling it with something that looked like salt but wasn't edible, ruining the dinner. Yes, as rational thinkers, we possess the gift of reason. The Creator made us be like Him. Because His understanding is endless, to think we can exclude the source of all knowledge in establishing our wisdom and logic is a mistake. How unintelligent is it to exclude the Originator of thought from the thought process itself? God said, "...let us reason together" (Isaiah 1:18). This passage shows God wants to communicate with us. He wants us to understand how He thinks so we can learn to know Him intimately. To exclude the possibility that God exists is to exclude the author of reason. Therefore, any conclusion we come to that is void of God's ability to influence humanity eliminates the only possible way to understand the meaning of life.

We base the knowledge of cosmogony on the data we call science. Physics and chemistry are two of the "hard" sciences, more amenable to analysis. This systematic branch of learning we call science is a fundamental acceptance of fair principles known by experience or observation. The basis of scientific fact is the ability to administer experiments in a closed environment. However, this type of investigation is challenging when dealing with the undocumented history of the universe.

Because humanity wasn't there in the unknowable past to document the origin of the universe, it is impossible to rule out God as the potential (*ex nihilo*) Creator of our space-time-matter reality. If the big bang explains the origin of the universe as we know it, what existed before the big bang? Unable to answer this question, science's laws relative to the source of the universe become theoretical assumptions supported by speculative philosophy. Science without the possibility of the existence of God is scientifically unprovable, and that aspect of knowledge becomes scientism. Unless you can include infinite principles in dealing with the known universe, you can only come to a finite conclusion. God's immeasurable understanding of all that exists is apparent in the Scriptures. The diversity of God's infinite wisdom manifested in and through His creation is viewable to humanity. The certainties of science can mislead when these accepted principles deny the possibility of a first cause (Matthew 24:4).

Words

Words help to live our lives. It is possible to communicate the principles of eternal reality truthfully with what we say, but we can establish finite deception as well (Ephesians 5:6). Because words are so influential, if someone misunderstands your point of view, what you say can cause someone to miss your true meaning.

If someone you trust miscommunicates with you, it can cause you to error from the truth. Sometimes false teachers will try to convince you to agree with something that opposes the Bible's teachings. The Devil himself can propose a lie shrouded with a semblance of truth by masquerading as an angel of light (2 Corinthians 11:14).

The Devil's secretive ability to use cunning and deceptive words to disguise his ornaments of desire is enormous. He is exceptionally resourceful in using his skills to get you to buy into some lie he communicates to you (2 Corinthians 11:3). Because of his influential abilities, it is dangerous to underestimate him. By using dishonest words, he completely deceived Eve in the garden scenario. Her deception was so complete he could get her to act contrary to what she knew to be right.

Satan, the great deceiver, was the first to fall prey to deception. He desires to discredit the deity of Jesus the Christ. However, no matter how great his deceptive abilities are, he can only do what we allow him to do. He roams the earth, casting a spell on everyone he can by physical, emotional, and spiritual means. If the Devil can keep the unsaved world from acknowledging the fact that he exists and from realizing who Jesus is, then deception remains. If he can prevent the church from understanding the authority of Christ, his powers remain intact. Adam gave up man's control over the world to Satan because he sinned. In Christ, the model of modest, obedient living, we have regained the authority to retake the ground Satan took from us.

Satan cannot read our minds, but he can determine what we are thinking by hearing what we say. Don't underestimate the power words have. Many curses in people's lives originated from their spoken word. The adage of sticks and stones can break my bones, but words will never hurt me is not valid, as misused words can hurt. They not only cause harm to others but can do significant damage to us as well. What we say determines hell's perception of influence in our lives. We can justify ourselves by speaking the truth or defile ourselves by speaking incorrectly (Matthew 12:37). We can also create physical consequences based on what we say.

Satan's intent through manipulation is to be our mouthpiece to exploit others. He attempts to get us to argue with each other at his level, thus rendering our work useless. Those who war with words are of no effect in advancing the kingdom of God (2 Timothy 2:14).

Our words can control people and change events in life. We can lose control of areas in our lives or protect areas of our lives with our speech. We can also develop a power of governance based on how we structure what we say. That is why attempting to justify your position using intimidation and manipulation to control a conversation is a cheap form of communication.

Not knowing the truth of the Bible could cause us to speak out of context. Our seemingly truthful words can take on false meanings. During the ages, the definition of specific terms has changed. Unless we know the Word of God, what we say can give the Devil a position of power to exploit us through dishonesty, allowing him to gain an advantage over us.

The expression of words can seem kind, but their intent can be one's selfish gain. They can sound sincere and confident but lack genuineness. If what you say is not honest, you will misrepresent spiritual truth. And it requires truthfulness to be one of Christ's ambassadors.

You can promise the simple-minded person a smooth monetary ride along the path of life, but the rocky road of misfortune could become a dead-end trail. Well-to-do words can promise the good fortune a person will travel a long distance to get, but poverty could be the actual destination of the journey.

Some people spend their entire lives trying to live up to the expectations of others. It's as if recognition from high-minded individuals validates the void in life we can all experience. However, we all know becoming famous and popular does not satisfy the desire to know your true self. If it did, there would not be many of the wealthy living shipwrecked lives despite their riches. Real meaning in life comes from developing the understanding that contentment comes from who you are and not what you accumulate. It understands that your intrinsic significance comes from knowing you are a child of God.

What we say can make things seem larger than life. Attempts

to increase oneself through hollow promises are of the very nature of Satan. Empty promises are what he proposed to the angels who fell with him and are the exact promises he made to Eve. Satan tries to excite our senses and make the lie seem attractive through false charm. Working through the fall, he directly attacks those who have avoided his confinement. Preventing unintended consequences in life requires breaking free of hell's grip and escaping.

It's okay to move with a sense of urgency to things said to us, but we should always be ready to listen. Like a judicial hearing, we should gather facts about the situation. We should allow people to finish their entire train of thought as uncontrolled speech or speaking in haste makes it possible for you to say something that is not entirely true or pertinent to the situation.

We should desire to add virtue and substance to others, improving their lives with what we say. Our terms should speak for themselves, with no need for defense. We should display spiritual insight with the clarity of intent, thus preventing the enemy from using how we communicate to harm others. Spiritual wisdom prohibits the enemy from using us. Do not put words to your negative thoughts.

Satan's descriptive definitions show the author's vile communication. We should not make false or harmful statements intending to cause someone grief. Even if the reports are accurate, they could damage an individual's reputation. Remain aware of the fact that there is only one accuser of the brethren. Therefore, prayer should always be the posture we should take regarding any disagreeable person we encounter.

Those who deceive others are, by their very act of deceiving, deceive themselves. Fabrication of truth through trickery is a profession that worsens with use. Such action can have the contrived effect that the snake charmer's murmurings have, causing the snake to yield its will to the charmer's false power.

Like an image in a looking glass, what we say should mirror the Holy Scriptures. If seen through the reflection of the Scriptures, we can keep accusations far from our conversations. We should not respond improperly and avoid attacking or defaming another's reputation by speaking secretly or whispering into the ear of another person. Proper discernment that causes you to have ill feelings toward another does not reflect the will of God for that individual. That's why the Bible should always be the standard-bearer for approved living.

We should not belittle the worth of someone through words based on falsely designed evidence. What we say should move forward in approval of those we encounter in life. We must keep from becoming hell's agents of accusation, not allowing inappropriate annoyances expressed through words to injure someone.

Even though we are familiar with God through experience and understanding His ways, we can neglect to honor Him in our everyday lives. Show through the excellence of conduct the worship, honor, and praise that God deserves. Successfully recognizing the importance of covering ourselves with the achievements of Jesus Christ keeps the will of hell from becoming a reality. Jesus earned the glory of His name. Being grateful to Him avails us of the protection that His name affords us. In doing so, we show our appreciation to God, who protects us through a life of thankfulness. In Jesus, we have avoided the hold of hell and should express happiness and gratitude because of what God has done for us. If we do not walk before God in an appreciative posture, our thoughts can lose their intrinsic meaning and become unsuccessful in achieving significant resistance to evil. Our thankless conduct can cause us to play the fool. We walk with little or no light at all if we cannot glorify God with thankfulness. We reveal the brightness of God through worship and thanksgiving. Worship protects our thoughts, and thanksgiving keeps us in the light.

Words designed through self-effort to increase one's stature are powerless to change a person's life properly. Without the empowerment that comes from God, what we say cannot intrinsically improve us. God does not operate apart from His word. His power created the universe. God's power and God's words are inseparable; thus, His power is never absent from His words; we cannot make them void.

Satan Accuses Us

Those who make a career out of accusation are familiar with the demonic method. Accusers understand hell's ways of communicating and approve the use of this habitual lifestyle. Since the creation of man, the Devil has been an accuser of men. There is no truth within his nature or in his vicinity. He treats all lies like his children, nurturing them, causing them to grow.

Satan wants to knock us around like the ball in a table tennis game. Do not wrestle with the enemy's inquiries by using unnecessary words. Satan usually has some indirect purpose in mind. Use a direct approach to resisting darkness. Just confess your sin, submit to God, and Satan will flee. God has communicated to us the victory we now have over our defeated foe. Satan no longer has direct access to our lives because of Jesus Christ.

He Afflicts Us Mentally and Physically

Jesus has given us victory over sin and diseases. He took upon himself the sin and sickness of the world. Circumstances do not reflect who we are. They do not represent our victory in Christ. When things go wrong in people's lives, it does not mean a person has fallen out of favor with Father God. Even though Satan can influence our circumstances, by correctly reacting to adverse events practically, we confirm the sufficiency of God's working power.

Success in life occurs in our spirit, not through our circumstances; through the daily grind of life, our relationship with the Holy Spirit continually strengthens us with the truth of the eternal gospel. This truth allows us to live with supernatural strength in our everyday affairs. Based on factual events, the cross itself seemed like a massive defeat. Circumstances do not define you; they reveal who you are.

The eternal destiny of a Christian is in Christ. Physical destruction is not eternal punishment. Only through the rejecting of the eternal Son of God is the soul of a human condemned to eternal damnation. Bowing the knee in fear of darkness is idolatry. But the fear of the Lord is the beginning of wisdom.

Being a Christian does not incubate you from aggravating circumstances. However painful or injurious existing conditions are in the life of a Christian, they are usually temporary. Sometimes the wounds or scars we sustain in life are signs of life. Hard times often draw you back to your heavenly Father.

During the frontier days of America, cattle ranchers would brand their cattle. These scars identified their cows. Should they mingle with another rancher's herd, each rancher always knew which cattle were his. When we suffer for Christ, He sees our wounds as identifying marks showing that we belong to Him.

Satan tries to use difficulties in life to squeeze the life out of us. He breaks us and gets us to change our lifestyle by making it seem like we will always be in a tight spot. If we worry about our circumstances, we usually try to solve problems with our strength. If he can, he will confuse us and make it difficult for us to stay focused on Jesus. It is imperative to remember that we will not lose out. Our reactions to difficult or troubling situations should always be the same as Paul's was in Philippians 4:13. Our hope is in Jesus, and through Him, we can do all things.

Satan treats us unfairly and cruelly, wanting us to be unhappy and live anxiously, intending to smite us and overtake us. He doesn't leave us alone. But neither does God. God will never give up on us. He will never abandon us when we go through tough times, even when nothing seems to go right. We may suffer severely, but God is always present. He saw it coming. He is ready to equip you to go through it; if we stand and remain obedient, God will never let Satan cause actual damage. Satan may cause us pain. But without God's permission, he cannot annihilate us.

As we move about in this life, carrying the message of Jesus Christ, one of our aims should be to render our carnal nature ineffective. We are to put to death the things that do not draw us closer to Jesus. We should show this newness of life through our actions. The resurrection power that raised Jesus from the dead quickens our mortal bodies. It should be clear to all that even though we are ordinary people, the power of God lives in us. Through the Holy Spirit, we overcome our fallen nature.

When we experience things that are beyond our control, it could feel overwhelming. However, God will use something we can't control to prove that He is an ever-present help in times of trouble. God uses these momentary light afflictions to produce everlasting strength in our lives. We should never think of ourselves as a failure. Things may seem cold and lifeless, and the surrounding stuff might be bothersome to you, but the inward interpretation of these things should stem from our renewed minds and regenerated spirits. The increase of God's life in us replaces the old process of living.

We experience our relationship with Jesus Christ in practical ways. We interact socially with supernatural powers made available to us because of our acquaintance with His divine power, like a legal contract written in heaven. Our relationship with Christ makes us able to serve others in practical ways. Whenever we do, we show Him the honor and respect He deserves.

We are to yield totally to the form of living that Jesus lived to be worthy of the calling of God in our lives. Often, we do not know what is going to happen to us. During these unknown times, we should remain calm and not fight against the purposes of Jesus, even if mistreated. We should feel fortunate and show great happiness when we come up to the batter's box for the Lord Jesus. Christ paid the full price for our salvation. What we suffer for Him has tangible value. It is the glory of being able to identify with His atonement.

We are not to condone sin in the life of a believer whom Satan wants to destroy. However, Christians who need to change their life-styles are not enemies of God but Christ-followers who need resto-ration. Discipline is often the intent of harsh circumstances. During severe training, what we learn should always be our focus. Extreme events can be a successful way of dealing with a problematic area in our lives that requires transformation. I call it the 2x4 process. Sometimes God has to hit us in the forehead with a 2x4 piece of lumber to get our attention. If we are obedient to God, even tempo-rary exclusion from fellowship turns out for our good. It is import-ant to remember that God turns Satan's aim and uses it for our good.

We need to learn to recognize when Satan attacks us so we can deal with it immediately. If we experience sickness or disease, Jesus desires to heal. God's timing is always now. Nothing should prevent us from taking back the ground that Satan has stolen from us. His attacks will not have a lasting effect if we can identify them and overcome them. Our permanent position is freedom in Jesus Christ, not the bondage of hell.

If, at this very moment, you need food, clothing, or a place to stay, remember this: Problems in life do not mean that God is not pleased with you. Some of the greatest saints suffered the most violent of circumstances. We should count it all joy. In everything we go through, we should give thanks. If we are in God's will, then we are victorious. Do not listen to the lies of the enemy. Maintain a heavenly vision. We need to look beyond our physical realities to live an abundant life. Life is more than food, clothing, and shelter. True riches lay in a living, loving relationship with Father God.

God wants to lift us beyond our circumstances into exceeding greatness. We base the quality of our life on revelation from and relationship to God, not the comforts of this life. Sometimes things in life can be a constant source of frustration. Rather than concentrating on removing such obstacles, we should focus on God's higher intent for us. His thoughts are higher than our thoughts. He knows what we need. He knows how to sustain us. His will for us is always His aim in everything we go through. Our eternal purpose is still what God is trying to work out. We are to maintain humbleness in our relationship with God. He sometimes accomplishes this humbleness through the physical affliction that He has designed for us.

However, sometimes we will experience things that are not judicially correct. We can sink to the deepest despair if we do not come to grips because not all that occurs in our life comes from God. Perilous times await last-day believers. The belief that God will prevent all calamities from coming our way may seem politically correct, but it is not scriptural. Remember our circumstances do not gauge who we are in Christ.

If challenging, dry times rob us of our joy and friends betray us, society rejects us, trouble comes upon us suddenly, and we walk through dry places; despised or separated from loved ones, we are not alone. Though the path that leads to life is difficult, God has promised to walk with us. He is ever-present to prevent genuine harm. We must look to Jesus, who, for the joy set before Him, endured the cross and suffered death as a villain. He looked at the cross' suffering with disdain, thinking very little of the disgrace and dishonor associated with the cross. Jesus did not recede from the mission of the cross because, in it, the cause and occasion of His joy emerged, the snatching of the saints of God out of Satan's grasp (Hebrews 12:2). He looked down the halls of time and saw a great harvest of souls who would believe in Him. He endured the cross because He saw you and me in the bosom of the Father. In Him, we live and move and have our being. In Him, we have the victory.

He Opposes Us

Just like Pharaoh, Satan tries to destroy the work of God (Exodus 1:15-22). But God has promised to go before us (Psalm 85:13). The battle is the Lord's (Isaiah 27:1). He wants us to fight in His strength (Isaiah 51:9). God opposes those who oppose us (Ezekiel 29:12-15).

We are to school those who place themselves in opposition to us with kindly gentleness (Titus 2:12). If we don't get them to change their minds now, it doesn't mean we are not planting seeds for future action (2 Corinthians 1:10). Knowledge of the truth usually comes in stages. Some who oppose us are prospective members of God's family (Romans 2:4). Results in ministry are God's responsibility (Philippians 2:13).

We stand before the Father spotless because of Jesus, our High Priest. The Hebrew meaning of the name Satan is "an adversary." It applies this term in a judicial sense, just like an opponent in a court of law. "Devil" is the Greek word for Satan, and it means "accuser." Satan's nature opposes, and his actions accuse. The transliteration of the word used for "opposing" in Zechariah 3:1, when the accuser stands opposed to us and resists our work, is "satan." Satan resists our efforts in ministry. He challenges us whenever he can, wanting to devour anything we accomplish for the Lord Jesus. He causes adversity, fights against us, and will always resist us. When we fall, Satan tries to make us seem disqualified. Our righteousness is in the Lord Jesus. His sinless perfection makes us worthy. Regardless of what happens, we are to stand against the works of darkness (Luke 21:36).

Like a brand in the fire, sometimes we get charred and burned. Parts of us can get scorched and scarred up badly, but in Christ, we are as white as snow (Isaiah 1:18). Satan fixes his sights on us, but God pushes hell away from us. God fights for us. He defeats the enemy's plan for us (Psalm 71:13). He removes the clothing of shame the adversary has for us and confuses his plans (Psalm 109:20,29).

We exchange our filthy garments for garments of praise (Psalm 30:11). We put on the Lord Jesus Himself as our covering (Romans 13:14). The blood of the Lamb cleanses us (Revelation 1:5).

I was a brand plucked out of the fire. The co-worker who introduced me to the gospel told me if anyone would not make it to heaven, it was I. I was such a radically wild teenager that I had to experience some extreme circumstances in my life for God to get my attention.

The first car I ever owned was a 1959 Porsche Roadster. I paid $1100 for it in 1973. Before coming to Christ, this car was like a god to me. The highest God had to take this false god away from me to get my devotions. One Saturday night, many of my friends from school went up Azusa Canyon near where I grew up, as we were having a big party in the mountains. Afterward, I attempted to drive down the narrow mountain road regardless of being severely intoxicated. As I traversed down the hill, I remember passing a van that seemed to move at an idle speed. Later, at the scene of the accident, the van driver told me he was going 50 mph. I passed him like he wasn't even moving. Moments later, after multiple wild turns, I lost control of my car and wrapped it around the mountain. The car looked like I had split it open with an old-fashioned can opener (see the back cover). Because I had the top down on the Porsche, I flew from the vehicle going approximately 80 mph. My friend who rode the car to a stop looked back and saw me lying on the pavement a couple of hundred feet back on the road. He ran to me and shook me uncontrollably.

I was unconscious and possibly dead. Before being revived, I remember envisioning the Devil arguing with the Lord over my lifeless body. Hell was accusing me of my sins and saying they deserved to take my worthless life with them down to the bottomless pit. I remember Jesus standing over me, putting His hand up in my defense and saying, "No, he is my chosen vessel." Afterward, my caravan of friends arrived at the scene, along with members of the Azusa Police Department. I remember frantically running around, yelling at the top of my voice, screaming that hell had tried to kill me, but Jesus had just saved my life. Scampering from friend to friend, telling them I was Christian and that God had just saved me, I also went to every single police officer and told them the Devil was real and that God had just kept me from dying. The police officers, who were all conversing with each other, did not know what to think. My friends thought all of this talk about Jesus was a ploy to keep the cops from arresting me for drunk driving. Although this was not my intent, it worked. The police told me they would not take me to jail if I promised them I would go straight home and see a doctor first thing in the morning, something I never did, even though I woke up the next day with a massive headache. That fateful night was December 29th, 1973.

I became a Christian that night I was nineteen years old. Before my conversion, I remember some of my colleagues betting on whether I would make it to my twenty-first birthday. They had a weekly running bet and drew lots every Friday to see who would cash in if I did not push through the weekend. Fortunately, God had an eternal purpose for me. His love and forgiveness are the most extraordinary things I have ever experienced.

He Hinders Us

Satan can alter our plans (Galatians 5:7). However, persistence will always lead to a breakthrough. We need to know what God has planned for us. Ignorance can lead to errors and mistakes. Wrong decisions can lead to unknown circumstances. Sometimes we cannot do the thing we set out to do. Hindrances can spring up and prevent us from making things happen. Just like a road that is impassable because of construction work, Satan tries to put roadblocks all over the path to God. He is relentless in his persistence to put obstacles in front of us. We need to determine where the hell is opposing us because he cuts into our lives to impede our course.

When we focus on God's will for our lives, Satan tries to distract us and get us to react to life's circumstances temporally. Because he is always trying to hinder our growth, we must be careful to understand our heart's condition.

Cosmic Domain

Jesus Christ created the known universe (Ephesians 3:9). It remains created because God wills it to (1 Corinthians 8:6). He sustains all that exists (Isaiah 40:12). He is the uncreated God who created everything (Psalm 102:25-27). The Father, Son, and the divine Spirit are the only uncreated beings in existence (Hebrews 1:10-12). Collectively, they are the Godhead. Together, through Son's agency, they have created all that exists (John 1:3). One of the significant reasons hell is furious with humans is that we are the crowns of the glory of God's creation. The Devil knows this because we are the ones through whom God has revealed His true wisdom (Ephesians 3:10).

Ranks and Power Levels of Wicked Spirits

Because of the cosmic rebellion in the heavenly realm, the spirit world contains good spiritual agents and evil spiritual agents. Initially, the magnificent creations of God, evil divine beings, are the consequence of wrong choices. The base of their terrible existence is an incorrect belief system that bought into the same lie that Lucifer did. We now know Lucifer as Satan, the chief prince of darkness. Although these divine beings are sinful, God uses them for good (Romans 8:28).

The Bible tells us that Michael and Gabriel were angels of a higher rank. Scripture also alludes to the fact that Lucifer was a divine being of rank. In the New Testament, the Apostle Paul tells us that there seems to be a semblance of order in the dark side of the spirit world. Whether this means a ranking of authority within the evil spirit world or not, there appears to be a strategic line of command, a military structure assigned to some darkness agents that oppose us.

The Bible also tells us we wrestle against these agents of darkness. A wrestling match is a contest between two opponents trying to gain an advantage over each other through the strategic positioning of oneself to throw the other off-balance. The goal is to achieve a decisive advantage as you try to pin your opponent to the mat by holding them down, rendering your opponent inoperative and unable to defend themself. If one person lets his guard down for an instant, he usually finds himself at a disadvantage because of his opponent's continual onslaught. Though the Bible defines our struggle with darkness as a wrestling match, it is not a game. It is a struggle between life and death (1 Timothy 6:12).

In the New Testament book of Ephesians chapter 6, these dark agents we wrestle against are identified for us. The Bible depicts these entities as evil, divine spirits, not terrestrial beings. Ephesians 6:12 (YLT) states, "Because we have not the wrestling with blood and flesh, but with principalities, with the authorities, with the world-rulers of the darkness of this age, with the spiritual things of the evil in the heavenly places." The Bible tells us that our enemies in the unseen spirit realm exist and are dangerous to humans. Again, although the Bible does not specify their rankings, if you look at them from a military perspective, you could say a principality is a general, authorities are like a colonel, a world ruler is like a captain, and the host of evil spirits or demons are like privates. The Bible describes these evil spirit beings as having micro and macro territorial authority and has examples of how these entities interact in our lives. If we do not adequately protect ourselves, these cosmic forces can require and receive your submission.

Principalities, commonly called cosmic powers, are high-ranking officials, supreme leaders in the dark world. They exercise authority, command, and have a dominating influence. They start many worldwide events that have adverse effects on humanity that infect global and individual everyday affairs. Like a judge in a court of law, they have legal jurisdiction to make judiciary decisions that affect entire regions. In the extreme sense of the word, they are very dangerous.

Another of the high-ranking officials in the hierarchy of hell is the powers, sometimes called authorities. These are spirits in authority but under a rule that governs over an area or group. These supernatural beings also have high-standing military and governmental authority; under the direction of regional principalities, they can still demand submission and obedience from large sections of humankind.

Because of their high rank of command, principalities and powers can perform what we might call miracles. Unlike God, they cannot create something out of anything. Their advantages are usually the manipulation of the natural processes of creation. Powers, like principalities, do not have the limitations of some lesser agents. Their rule's splendor is mighty, and with authority to influence as they see fit, they are the more powerful evil entities that infect mortals.

Rulers of darkness are what we might call the warlords of the spirit world. Their assignment is to darken people's minds, blinding humans to the affairs of the netherworld. Making the misery of hell a reality in people's lives, they promote ungodliness and immorality. Just like a person whose eyes are blinded but eventually adjust to the darkness in a movie theatre, they make a person's vision adjust to the dark surroundings of life created by their influence. They expect us to believe their darkened fallen world is ordinary.

Spiritual hosts of wickedness are what we would call foot soldiers or the infantry. These are the ones who create havoc in your daily walk with Christ. They promote malice, depravity, iniquity, and vice. Even though they are the boots to the ground regiment, they are more potent than unprotected men, but they are inferior to God. The entire demonic hierarchy is subservient to God and can serve God's greater purpose for His creation.

Our spiritual battle is against these supernatural beings bent on destroying us. The battle station of these creatures is in the atmosphere surrounding the earth. Because they are spirit beings, as we understand it, space and time do not limit them. As divine spirits, they can move freely and travel long distances quickly. They can pounce on us from above, continually bombarding our minds with their evil intentions as they work from the airwaves over the earth.

Agents of Darkness

Romans 8:38-9. The reference here is what can sever us from the love of God. Nothing created can.

Of all these divine evil beings, the one that animated the serpent in the garden scene seems to have taken center stage in the battle raging on for the lives of humanity. Satan, the name given to this adversarial accuser of humankind, seems to have achieved paramount significance in the realm of these fallen beings. He rules and reigns over most of their affairs. His authoritative command renders final decisions. Like Michael is in the heavenly sphere, Satan is to the netherworld. His residence is foremost in location and was the divine being who started legal action against humanity. As the princely power and supreme overlord of his deceptive clan, Satan has become the official chief of darkness. He functions like the warden of a prison whose guards try to keep their population captive. He is their commander in chief and functions as an overseer of the other classes of darkness.

However, regardless of rank or power, these evil spirits are subject to Jesus Christ (Colossians 1:16), who sets at the highest place of honor (Ephesians 1:21), the right hand of Father God (1 Peter 3:22). The throne of God is the domain of Jesus Christ. All wicked spirits are subordinate and under Him (Philippians 2:9-11). They must obey and yield to Him. Just like military troops under the command of their leader, their freedom has limitations, as darkness must heed the will of God in the name of Jesus. They must cooperate and are subject to the authority of God. Jesus, the great Deliverer, has saved us from the dangerous position of Satan's control (Colossians 1:13).

When we become Christians, we lose our right to live independently from God (Romans 6:13). This loss of independent status makes us worthy of the name of Jesus. By laying aside our lives, we establish an intimate relationship with Jesus Christ. Like a life separated from its natural existence, we are to live a life consecrated to God. We are to give ourselves into His hands, allowing God to take care of us and manage our affairs. We commit our lives to God, who molds them as He sees fit. When we experience the life of Jesus in this mortal existence, we present ourselves as His to keep and do as He pleases. The fullness of life comes from God. The genuine vitality of actively living a life devoted to God is essential in experiencing the fullest blessings available to us in this existence.

Hell Deceives the Entire World

As Christians, we know what it means to have an encounter with God. We have discovered through revelation, examination, and personal inspection that Jesus is Lord. We have perceived the fact that the recognition of the existence of God gives us understanding. The condition of our lives and the state in which we live, based on the knowledge of God's presence, have given us definite meaning, and we know what we must do about it. Unlike a non-Christian, we have discernment regarding the things of God (1 John 5:19). The earth inhabitants who live ungodly lives keep their hostility to religious affairs in this alienated state of mind through Satan's influence (Ephesians 4:18). Satan puts hindrances in people's lives through frail and fleeting desires and pleasures that prevent people from accepting Christ's cause (2 Corinthians 4:4). Covering up the truth, trying to influence people into making a stand against the ways of God, the Devil tries to set things in motion designed to lay a foundation of lies, making people subject to his ways. He uses annoyances, hardships, and pressured situations to cause pain and trouble. He tries to get people to think that Christianity's faith and steadfastness are not the answer needed to withstand his evil, wicked ways.

Like a God

For a period in this present reality, Satan conducts his affairs like a god. He tries to resemble the true God in any way he can through his attempts to represent himself as the Highest God. He attacks the processes and purposes of our thoughts in his efforts to keep us from being able to discern the things of God by darkening our minds. By becoming insensitive to God's concerns, we can lose the ability to understand the knowledge of truth in its purest sense. The power to understand moral and spiritual truth is a delicate quality that only God can reveal. As Christians, we see God's representation in the person of Jesus Christ, which transforms us into this supreme likeness. We apply this truth based on the power of Christ's divine nature and His association with humankind. Satan covers up this truthful revelation in the lives of those who reject the truth of the gospel. The fact of God shines forth and radiates from His throne. Satan tries to prevent our reasoning from experiencing this act of enlightenment by choosing incorrectly. If, through deception, Satan can open a door in our lives, then it darkens our understanding.

Life's Meaning

I have concluded that logic and reason are not logical or reasonable. If God exists, then He is the author of life. If the last cause of reality, the supreme culmination of everything that is, that which is more significant than us, is someone or something other than the personal and infinite God of the Bible, then finite reasoning is logical. However, if an infinite final cause created man in His image, it is not rational for man to exclude Him. If God is the infinite, ultimate cause of the universe and is the Creator of all that exists, to exclude Him in our reasoning is the exclusion of that which gives meaning to logic and reason. Designed to replicate the divine infinite being of the universe, God made us rational, freethinking moral agents. Based on our individual choices, we create our realities relative to our destinies. I have already discussed how important to God's economy the existence of free will is. God asks us to reason with Him, not to remove the possibility that He exists from our thought processes.

Creation is but an immeasurable fraction of the reality of God's understanding. God's existence is being everywhere present, knowing everything knowable, and sustaining everything that exists merely by willing it. I am divinely favored beyond measure to know that the crowning recognition of man's ability to conduct himself intelligently is complete when we give God His rightful place in our lives. We understand Satan is merely a created being, and the Creator has endowed us with divine authority to defeat the darkness in our lives, enabling us to live victoriously. To believe is to know. To know is to believe. The crowning glory of the mystery of God's miracle is coming face to face with His loving Son, who has re-established our completeness through the power of the presence of His loving Spirit. To think that God (in all the greatness that makes up His countenance) presents Himself to humanity as a loving Father is overwhelming. Deep down in my spirit where, by faith, God dwells, there is a river of joy that can only find its origin in the realm of the divine. It is overwhelming to know that God has established a relationship with me through His begotten Son, Jesus Christ. To recognize that God loves me and cares enough about me that if I were the only person ever created, He would still have had an eternal purpose for me is incredible. Christ was the lamb slain from the foundation of the earth, thus reconciling me back to the Father. It is beautiful to know that God's love protects my life, like any good parent does for their child.

As a child of the King, I stand in the full authority of God in my life. I have the keys to withstand the lies of my soul's enemy because I am hidden in Christ. I have overcome by Christ's blood and by my testimony lived out in practical ways. Christianity is not illogical. It is, in fact, the most logical conclusion to life. It is unbelievable what a person needs to believe to be an unbeliever. Without God, the evolutionary process of natural selection takes the real meaning out of life. It takes more faith to make truth relative, deny that something divinely inspired the Bible, and that God exists than it does to believe in the Bible narrative and the God who authored it. Over forty authors wrote the Bible's sixty-six books over 1500 years across three continents in three different languages. Yet, it is scientifically accurate, both numerically and historically. The encapsulated theme of the entire Bible is Jesus Christ, the Savior of humanity. This actual reality is His story communicated to us. He has made His presence knowable and has made a way of escape reconciling us back to the Father. He has made it possible for us to re-establish God's authority in our lives. The gospel lifts the veil. It re-establishes God's sovereignty in a person's life.

Faith gives birth to God's authority in your life. Authority gives birth to God's love in your life. And God's love changes your life. The consummate revelation of God's sound wisdom has endured the test of time, lining up with truth and fact alike. His understanding promotes wholesome living. It also embraces integrity and leads us into a healthy lifestyle. God's wisdom possesses the ability to repair, restore, and refresh us when things go awry.

By confidently trusting in the truth, we come to know the direct meaning of God's words to us by learning to understand Jesus' teachings. God's thoughts through revelation and instructions in His written Word given to us denote the essence of His wisdom as manifested in Jesus Christ. The Word of God persuades our inner-self that God entrusts, saving faith to the character and work of Jesus Christ. Jesus Christ is without beginning or end. His ceaseless life is the inheritance of those who believe (John 6:47). Separation from the life in Jesus sentences you to damnation and eternal punishment (Matthew 25:46). Hell is total separation from God. The complete absence of His presence. Christ transforms us from eternal separation from God into His abundant reality (John 3:36).

Because we carry this treasure in earthen vessels, we should not feel guilty or uncomfortable if we lack the skill to proclaim the truth of the gospel. We should not get anxious and worry about our effectiveness. The anointing comes from God (Acts 9:22). The power of Jesus in us exerts His force in proclaiming His truth (John 15:4-5). Jesus infuses the strength and ability to influence the gospel; because of the working of grace, we do not base it on effort. As A. W. Pink stated, "We are preserved from our enemies and delivered safely, from the penalty, power, presence, and pleasure of sin" (individually). God saves separately, one person at a time. He has made His salvation available collectively to everyone but communicates it to each person personally. God has no grandchildren. Every one of us must choose to accept His loving grace. When someone believes the gospel is accurate, they reap the benefits of salvation (John 5:24).

If Satan's attempts to hinder the gospel by hiding its true meaning are successful, many people will die in sins. However, whenever someone desires to turn their lives around and worships the true God in loving obedience like a little child, God's righteousness and wisdom open to them. Truth takes away that which surrounds and envelops their lives, wrapping their consciousness with guilt and sin, allowing them to see the glad tidings of salvation through Jesus Christ and His Word for the first time in their life. His (Jesus') death to sin for all humanity and His resurrection from the dead is the majesty of God made manifest to humankind.

As we mature into our knowledge of this truth, we become steadfast and immovable in our faith. We become strong because the nourishment we receive is powerful enough to sustain us. Completeness, wanting nothing, is necessary to mature in integrity and virtue. During tough times, we grow because of our ability to act and to choose correctly. Through practice, we develop habit patterns based on external conduct, which involve using our senses. By holding to the truth in our minds, our behavior becomes closely joined to the person of Jesus Christ. We strengthen our bond with Him as we walk out our faith. Our ability to perceive and understand the things of God enables us to judge correctly. With vigor, we should exercise our ability to know the truth without restraint. By taking advantage of our increased capabilities and continue to draw near to Him, we differentiate both good and evil. We should embrace those things, which are valuable and commendable, competently honoring the Lord while comforting others and confirming the Word implanted in us, which can save our souls. Identify items that are troublesome and eliminate them from our conduct and our thought life.

The gospel makes us ready for service by opening the mind's faculties, making us able to know the truth that sets us free. It enables us to change how we live, thus realizing the origin of separation from union and fellowship with God begins in our thoughts, which leads to conduct blinded by darkness. The gospel moves us towards the light. The spiritual truth of God's power to change a person's life comes from the heavenly influence that changes our understanding.

Before the gospel, ignorance of the ways of God darkened our understanding of divine things. But when the light of the Word of God presents itself, it exposes its true meaning for all to see. The sovereign power of God in the person of Jesus possesses the ability to control the things that belong to Him, thus conforming us into the image of Jesus Himself. This earth and everything on it belongs to God (Psalm 24:1). He has made ways for us to succeed in Him by using opportunities through His eternal plan for our lives. He regulates life. We change our conduct based on the power of God's life passed onto us in Jesus Christ. Like a parent welcoming a newborn baby, He has transferred His name to us intimately. Like parents who trust their child with all the identity and benefit of a relationship formed in love, He instructs us. He nourishes us by molding our lives into His loving likeness with an inheritance waiting for us in heaven.

We are to move away from the things that occupied our lives before conversion. Just like a lamp lights up a room, we should shine brightly as children of God. We are to cause places and people to brighten up by the truth in us as this brightness reflects the gospel's message. The very center of our lives should reflect the light of God (Ephesians 5:8). Our character and actions should affect other people's passions and desires toward the Lord. Intelligently, the gospel directs people to live lawful and morally right lives through the understanding that comes from advanced learning. The gospel possesses the ability to lead us to the right choices based on in-depth knowledge and experience of the things of life. The gospel belongs to God. His kingly majesty is revealed, and the splendor and brightness of God's countenance as supreme ruler and holy one is manifested to us. Through the blessedness that comes from knowing Jesus Christ as Savior and the soon coming King, God reveals His inward thoughts and feelings towards us. As shown by His view of humanity, Christ's treatment of man has made us joint-heirs of God in Christ. Indeed, we are seated in heavenly places in Christ Jesus.

The places in our lives we value are where Satan tries to continue to hold on to us. He wants us to develop his survival methods. He covers up the truth to prohibit the removal of that portion of our life that positions itself against the ways of God. To validate our lives based on living arrangements in the old manner of thinking keeps us from finding the revelation in Jesus Christ. The influence and power of Christ sever us from our old ways and separates us from our old modes of thinking into the newness of life. The effect and energy that come from the gospel abolish the old ways of living, removing the old lifestyle's futile efficiencies once and for all. Based on Jesus, this is our current state of affairs.

The gospel of Jesus Christ makes what we say, how we act, and what we do brand new. This transition from hell's kingdom to God's kingdom removes former restrictions. Dedication to the renewing process of the gospel cleanses us from wicked ways, purifying us from the guilt of sin, rendering us righteous. In the activity of the Holy Spirit, we walk out into this novel way of living. The very breath that proceeds from us should reflect this unique nature.

If we fall by the wayside of life, finding ourselves wandering, deviating from the truth, God in His infinite mercy draws us back to Him. God causes energy to be refreshing, exciting, and strengthening us through the spiritual power that gives us an increase; He restores us to life by quickening our new spirits. Before conversion, we were lifeless, destitute, and spiritually dead; at the cross, God rendered our sinful nature inactive, thus preventing it from operating.

There was a time when the operative forces of this life were at work in us, putting forth the power of the evil influence of darkness. As if we were the progeny of the Devil himself, we used to live contrary to the will of God. Determined to act unreasonably and desiring not to change, we placed a high value on adorning ourselves with the ornaments of this life.

Like those who consciously choose to defy Him, every one of

us has turned away from God in our sinful longings for the forbidden craving for our old fallen nature. Functioning in selfishness, the promise of the lie led us astray, making opposition to God seem normal. Our natural dispositions and impulses can inflict the wrath of God if left unchecked. But God, who supplies us from the greatness of His resources, gives us virtue and eternal treasures.

By experiencing the pain of the just punishment we deserve, God shows us kindness under our circumstances. In His divine providence, through the work of Jesus, God helps us despite our bent to sinning. He made the way of reconciliation possible in Himself. God reveals the many beautiful moments of experiencing the fact that God highly favors us in the gospel message of Jesus Christ. To entertain the thought that God is fond of us and loves us dearly gives us peace and allows us to be content with and to welcome the things that cross our path in this life. We dwell in the presence of the loving affections of the God of the universe, who loves us enough to die for us.

The Bible declares that to become a part of the family of God, you must be born again. Before a person comes to a saving knowledge of Jesus Christ, they must grip the reality that their sin separates them from God, that their spirit possesses none of the authentic living characteristics required to live relationally with the Lord. Our spiritual condition has suffered the impoverishment cast upon us by our sin. Like being on our own, homeless, without food, money, or possessions, we meander from home to home, seeking refuge. Despite this unacceptable living condition, when we become a follower of Jesus, God showers us with the eternal riches of His Son (Ephesians 1:3). The gospel of Jesus Christ reveals to us the value of our true nature through the abundance of the gospel.

God's holy influence in Jesus enables us to receive the divine benefits of His favor. His loving grace compensates us with the generous kindness of His goodwill. Grace rescues us from the danger and destructiveness of our evil ways.

I do not see mortal death as prolonged death. It is but the beginning of divine life. God has caused us to experience a new life based on the principles of eternity. This new life lifts hell's grasp in Jesus, the Son of God, the Savior of humankind, God incarnate and places us in the bosom of God Himself. This actual state of redemption dedicated to God is not obtainable through human effort.

God's grace reconciles us back to Father God. We find restitution acceptable to God in the life of Jesus. He is the substitute who took the place of judgment our sins deserved. Nothing we could ever do can pay the price for our sins. God withholds judgment only when we put our faith in Jesus. At conversion, our life begins afresh with the renovated cleansing that restores us to a completely alternative way of living. The Holy Spirit fuels this conversion process. The Holy Spirit is the third person of the triune God of the Bible who communicates the gospel of Jesus Christ to humanity. Therefore, we should object to the suggestions of darkness and restrict hell's ability to derail us.

We should not sink back into our old way of living (Galatians 5:1). True liberty is living as we should, not as we please. We should put on the provision of God based on reverent conduct. The salvation of Yahweh is in the "anointed One." Do not construct instruments that will provide our selfish desires to produce for their actions that lead us away from the grace of God. We should not plan our future with provisions that prevent us from receiving the fullness of God's grace as expressed in the gospel. Hell wants us to act under its capacity to corrupt God's plan for us. Despite a propensity to sin, we must equip ourselves with the ability to resist hell fighting against the firm and seemingly uncontrollable desire to do evil. In His great love, God, who is rich in mercy, has made a way of escape so we can stand against the wiles of the Devil. Glory to Jesus the Christ, who deserves all the credit and praise because He has reunited us back to our original state of inheritance. We are co-owners of the things of God because of His eternal purpose, which He purposed in Jesus Christ. The gospel sets us free. It lifts the veil of darkness, allowing us to see clearly into the realities beyond this existence. It confirms that God loves us and will sacrifice everything at His disposal to restore us to the right relationship with Himself.

If you were to take part in a mud-wrestling match, your clothes would become so dirty and soiled that you wouldn't want to wear them in public. The first thing you would do after the game is to peel those filthy clothes off and head straight for the shower so you could remove the filth from your body. After you finish your shower, you'd put on clean clothing. The gospel of Jesus Christ is like taking off those filthy clothes, like being cleansed by taking a shower in the Holy Spirit to clean and purify you. Spiritually, that is what the gospel does. Your righteousness is as filthy rags before you come to the saving knowledge of Jesus Christ. Afterward, you put on the new-ness of life in the Lord Jesus and experience a new birth to cleanse your sins by faith, thus making them white as snow.

CHAPTER 6:

CHURCH UNDER SIEGE

Hell's minions' attack on the church is continuously taking place. After a person becomes a Christian, it transfers him from the kingdom of darkness into God's family of divine light. Throughout history, this transforming act in the lives of humanity is the overall intent of the Highest. I previously mentioned that this transformation alerts hell. Immediately, hell's dark forces are bent on destroying our effectiveness. Hell ever struggles to get us to conclude that Christianity is not the road to redemption by trying to blind us to the works of God. They oppose, seduce, mislead, oppress, vex, afflict, and try to hold us captive in every way possible. Their apparent assaults are the least effective. It is the attacks wrapped with normalcy and less obvious that cause the most damage in our lives.

God has chosen us; we did not choose God; He has revealed His truth to us. As truth lays out the directions of life and expresses the will of God, Scripture has all the information we need to live in victory. Commit to memory the things God has recorded on our behalf. He has documented the formula designed to prevent hell from knocking us off our mark. The Word of God is the ultimate authority of the things of darkness. It communicates the power and provision needed to resist the enemy of our souls. Just listening to or reading God's Word is not enough to develop a complete understanding of the provision it avails. The Holy Spirit must make the truth known.

To grasp the truth, one must press into the things of God. It is wise to preface any time spent in the Bible to request that the Holy Spirit open up our understanding of the revelatory truths it contains. To develop an understanding of the way of salvation revealed in the Bible is the beginning of comprehending the intrinsic spiritual perspective of divine reality. It is essential to do the items outlined in the Scriptures that allow you to understand God's things. Otherwise, the Devil will come in and snatch away what you have learned.

God also speaks to us through the Holy Spirit. The Holy Spirit affirms the written Word. He encourages, advises, and directs us in the things of God. Evil spirits also attempt to communicate to us. They wander the earth, trying to lead us astray. Like the traveling salesperson of old, these imposters roam from town to town to keep from being detected, influencing through lying precepts. They cause us to error from the truth.

They Hold Captive

Sobriety is a state of mind in full command of its faculties. To yield to the Devil dulls your spiritual senses, affecting the ability to conduct oneself safely, similar to an intoxicated individual. When we least expect it, Satan likes to take captive those genuinely alive through a relationship with Jesus Christ. The path of life is full of his tactics, attempting to entangle us in the affairs of this world. Satan uses the allurements of this life to trip us up and get us to sin. His sudden and deliberate attacks can capture the believer and make them think they are making their own choices by design. When in reality, they are acting out the wishes and predetermined plans of darkness.

Satan constantly challenges us, attempting to derail our faith. If he can convince humankind that Christianity is a counterfeit life-style, he can maintain his control over the world. Ever trying to ruin the reputation of Christians, his goal is to discredit them by exploiting their failures. He wants us to question God and ourselves by convincing us that a character flaw keeps us from having a rela-tionship with God. If you are a Christian and you experience some type of failure, it does not disqualify you from your destiny. You do not fall in and out of favor with God when you miss the mark be-cause the forgiveness of Jesus safeguards your life. No one becomes a Christian with a legitimate claim to the acceptance of God. Before coming to Christ, we were like illicit children. Nothing in us merited the family relationship required for salvation. Therefore, hell always tries to make it seem like we serve God without a legitimate claim or that the only reason we are Christians is because of its benefits. Of course, as Christ's ambassadors, we need to exemplify commend-able conduct that expresses genuine repentance. But if we fail, it is essential to remember that Jesus did not!

With everything that God made being excellent and evil seeming so prevalent these days, it seems unreasonable not to consider that some type of consorted force is not at fault (2 Thessalonians 2:9). All the evil that exists confirms the dynamic nature of the evil one coming down from his throne, efficiently infecting people's minds. He has powers of influence superior to those of mere mortals and uses these powers to attack individual Christians and entire congregations. He collectively uses everything in his ability to impact all walks of life. With his vantage point in the second heavens, he has watched all cultures develop, making it possible for him to influence every group of people.

Satan uses all of his ability and influence to persuade us to revive our dead sinful natures and make it appear like it's okay to stray from our destiny. He will do whatever it takes to gain an advantage over you and prevent you from reaching out to a dying world. By initiating everything that finds itself opposed to God's works, he consciously opposes the church. In his attempt to violate the laws and the justice of God, he wants to render the church ineffective, preventing us from receiving supernatural help from God. If he can divide and break up the church's unity, he can deny us access to the throne room of heaven. If the church becomes fragmented, it cannot promote the reality of God's affections. Sentiments that save us from the evils that obstruct the reception of the gospel of Jesus Christ.

Satan tries to use the very circumstances we currently find ourselves in to defeat us. Therefore, we must learn to discern the enemy's ways. We must be mature in our understanding, so they do not treat us as if we are not of age in our knowledge, rendering us unable to resist the Devil's tactics. God wants us to cry out to Him so He can come to our aid when afflicted by demons that want to make us miserable. God does not want us to be under the power of demons. He wants us to position ourselves in such a way that we come to realize His protection. A child, not knowing it is resisting what is best, will throw a tantrum to keep from doing what is being asked of them. Likewise, an immature opinion that is contrary to the truth can easily lead a person astray. Hell uses misguided emotions against one who cannot understand the fact through lack of experience. If we fail when attacked, we must return to God and meet the conditions required to stop hell's influence in our lives.

The Devil comes into the church secretly attempting to destroy God's work, not wanting anyone to know what he is trying, thus seeing his activity. He is continually working to steal away the kingdom of God's progress by destroying the liberty a genuine believer has, making it seem like he is falling in and out of salvation through works. His intent is to deceive us into thinking the love relationship we have in Christ is not any more vital than the last sin we committed. He tries to break our lasting relationship with God by bringing us into bondage. He tries to enslave us by creeping in and damaging our lives through wrong thoughts and actions to get us to gamble with our lives and wander from the way's protection.

Satan can use those in the church who use their abilities to gain admiration from others but lack true piety to pollute our walk. The Devil wants us to live under his control, using his methods to tire us out with meaningless tasks. He desires to exhaust our efforts in labors that produce no fruit. It is imperative to remember God has provided the power that lives in His very nature for our defense, the ability that lives in the Holy Spirit. God's Spirit walks with us. The Holy Spirit encapsulates us from satanic oppression. Satan wants to rule over us and prevent us from realizing the opportunities we have at our disposal, making us vulnerable to his craftiness. He does not want us to experience the freedom that comes from yielding to the strength of the Holy Spirit.

There Are Footholds and Strongholds of Influence

Satan's influence varies in degree. However, his goal is to gain as much control as possible. He is always looking for ways to put obstacles in our path by arresting significant areas of our lives. Satan tries to get right in the middle of our dealings with God. When hell breaks out, we will feel its effect. When he frustrates our plans and causes things to get heated in our lives, he will try to create a smokescreen to prevent detection. We need to develop an awareness of the situations that hell uses against us to determine where Satan is working. We must know where his influence starts and how he got the legal right to influence us. By directly properly opposing him, he must leave or reveal the reason he can stay. Jesus did not come to "be served" but to serve and give His life a ransom for others (Matthew 20:28). God provided the victory in Himself (Jeremiah 31:11).

Demons will gang up on people. Like a lynch mob that is out of control, they usually accomplish what they set out to do. Unless we learn to stop the uproar, demons can excite trouble. They love to afflict the people of God, attempting to prevent virtuous conduct. They will use any annoyances possible to prevent us from serving God. Their stagnant ways try to stop us from experiencing the transforming power of God. A demon's plan to thwart us will be successful if he can keep us from withstanding the test of time. That's why it is imperative to leave our sinful carnal natures crucified to the cross because hell specializes in attacking our weaknesses. He will try to get us to function in a survival mode. If we wage war against hell using carnal, fleshly instruments, we provide Satan with an occasion to assign darkness agents to us. We must consecrate our physical bodies and entrust our souls to the Father. Satan will try to put a curse of death upon us. But if we have wholly surrendered our life to Jesus, our life is in God's hands.

They Afflict

When God appoints us to the office of His kingly court, He reveals His intentions for us. One of which is the ability to withstand darkness through self-control and guarded thoughts. We must wrap the inclinations of our inner man in righteousness to be agreeable to the Father. Our walk must be pleasant to the Father, perfect and complete. In humility, we must fit ourselves with the righteous garments of Jesus. We need to continue moving towards God without wavering or turning away. Realizing our position and standard of living result from the level of victory that Jesus got for us, we must not think we can stand on our own. Be careful of subtly moving away from the things of God, believing that hell will not notice because Satan will. Correct and just living enables God's protection. God is the ruler and judge of all the spirit world. He alone possesses the supreme authority to command. Choose to maintain His covering in our lives and depart from evil, avoiding those things that make it easy to remove us from God's presence and protection. To live independently of God is a condition that gets uncontrollably worse and eventually leads to eternal separation from God.

If God reaches down from heaven and takes from us, know it is for our best good. Do not bow the knee to the evil one and his ways just because things don't work out the way we think they should. Prohibit his (the Devil's) work by holding onto the truth without compromise. In absolute integrity, stand against the onslaught of hell, knowing God protects us. Satan is always looking for a way to penetrate the protective covering of God's judicial umbrella. He wants to invade our safe dwelling of fellowship, but we still prosper with the Lord, as God will always provide breakthrough (Romans 9:16). Hell knows this and tries to figure out how to thwart our prosperity. He will even try to incite the hand of God against us. However, if allowed to do so, God will use Satan's influence to try us. He purifies our character through our circumstances. If darkness penetrates a person's life yielded to Jesus, that person's best interest is always God's intended outcome. Troublesome circumstances can arise out of nowhere. Because of these circumstances, we might not be sure if God is happy with us. If you are a child of the King, the enemy of your soul is but an instrument of improvement in God's hand. God wastes nothing, using every opportunity to bring us closer to Him. Conformity to the image of His Son Jesus is God's primary motivation in His dealings with us.

God is proud of us. As a Father with a tender heart who wants to let everybody know He has the most incredible kids on earth, He enjoys showing us off, thus letting hell understand that the power of the cross of Christ working in us is sufficient. He loves to see us grow stronger and stronger, prevailing in hardships. We need to learn to put forth the strength of God's provision against Satan and develop our understanding that hell cannot destroy us without God's permission. It may seem like hell is swallowing us up, but God, who is always in control, is aware of Satan's actions. Satan introduces evil to us in hopes we will choose to violate God's laws, thus enabling him to advance against us. Even though the Devil tries to destroy all of our intimate relationships with those we love in Christ, he can do nothing he does not have the legal right to do. That's why it is vital to realize our legal rights and take judicial authority over the challenging areas of our life.

Though Satan can execute his power against our physical circumstances, he does not have the liberty to deprive us of life. We can prevent him from controlling us. If he lays claim to areas of our lives, we open ourselves up to pain inflicted illicitly. Remember he can only do to us what he has the legal right to do. Satan must refrain from inflicting harm unless he has the opportunity from God's design or our wrong choices. Satan wants to change our life's framework by weakening our strengths, hardening our hearts, and drawing first blood in his battle with us as he invokes evil upon us. He wants us to blame God for his assaults, wanting us to complain to God by affecting our lives' exterior appearances. We should never become indifferent to the works of God. He is an ever-present help in times of trouble.

If you are amid hard times in your life right now, Satan wants you to dwell on your experiences' negative aspects so you will live a fragmented life. He wants you to think you are not worth the effort it would take for God to intervene on your behalf. God wants to restore the broken pieces of our lives and reestablish us. We should never give up because Satan's attacks are like the destructive force of a missile in the heat of battle. He attacks both our physical and spiritual states of being. His physical attacks can penetrate our nervous system and burden us with various physical hardships. If our outward impulses give him access, he can infiltrate our physical bodies with infirmity. He can also try to take away the vigor of our souls by negatively affecting our passions. But we must maintain the wholesomeness of living.

To live a quality life, we must fulfill all the intentions of God for us. Jesus Christ reinstates the originally sanctioned condition of our nature that existed before the fall. Now, with the entirety of our being, we can walk before God in uprightness. Remember Christ died for the ungodly (Romans 5:6). We should never sink so low that we don't reach out to God for the help needed to maintain honorable living. We do not have to bring excessive trouble to our souls. God wants us to be free of hindrances that keep us from our eternal destinies, filling our lives with spiritual and physical blessings.

Our consciousness should not be void of understanding the ways of God. It is unwise not to use discretion—irrational thinking breeds words of indiscretion. Rash decisions will always lead to more frustration. Commendable conduct in troublesome, disagreeable times is the correct result of quality living. We must not transgress God's laws through disobedience because demons can affect us.

If allowed, they infect us using the abilities of hell that are at their disposal. A person can fall under the influence of demons in various ways; they penetrate our lives through ignorant or knowable sin; they can also access our lives through our ancestors' sins. Past trauma or tragedy can also open doors for darkness. Satan himself is probably never going to confront any of us individually. He doesn't need to assault us directly. Besides, we probably aren't that important to him. He has countless dark agents at his disposal to assist him in wreaking havoc in our lives. They have many tasks. Their goal is to defeat us by getting us to sin. Then, when they accomplish this task, they try to keep us from confessing our sins. If we confess our sin, they accuse us and try to embarrass us or humiliate us by making us feel cheap for failing.

They attempt to gain access to our lives through their many activities associated with the natures attached to the minions of hell. They vary significantly in identity and function according to their assignments and many unique job descriptions. Like lawyers who specialize in specific areas, these monsters focus on their particular areas of influence. They wrestle against us in groups, just like a tag team wrestling event. For instance, let's say you struggle with anger. A spirit of violence can attach itself to that emotion in a fit of rage and cause you to act even more violently than you usually would. Then, when your fever is over, the spirit of anger can move off the scene and give the nod for a spirit of condemnation to come in and rail on you and make you feel defeated. Then that spirit, when finished, can bring in a spirit of despair or hopelessness and lie to you about your worth or your ability to overcome the failures in your life. Moods of self-pity or pride can come in and finish that attack with a knockout blow to the head, with feelings of pridefulness masquerading as humility. Finally, a spirit of murder might try to convince you to commit suicide. While all of this is going on, you mistakenly think you are damaged goods when, in reality, they are the ones causing the damage. They take turns punching you and hitting you when you are down. If you let them, they can beat you up as severely as any physical beating can. After the assault, you feel defeated because you have left your emotions open to the enemy's attacks. Eventually, those spirits back off and wait for something else to pop up in your life so they can start the process all over again. If you continue to choose incorrectly, then the foul spirit comes in and starts battling with you all over again. So unless you stop the darkness, your life can experience violent up and down emotions. This roller coaster ride can deflate you and prevent you from enjoying victory in Christ Jesus. The irony is this victory is already ours. But unless we activate our success, it lies dormant, unable to assist us.

God wants us to stand against darkness and push the hell out of our ways of life. He has given us the tools, but He will not let us sit passively on the sidelines while He fights for us. It does not work that way. He wants to defeat the enemy in our lives through our actions. We are to stop hell by actively engaging in the battle using His battle plan. Many evil spirit names associate with emotional disorders. There are spirits of lust, anger, depression, doubt, unbelief, abuse, seducing, and deceiving, to name a few. Darkness takes on many specific identities, designed to attack us, particularly to parlay our weaknesses based on man's fall to defeat and ultimately to destroy us utterly. Jesus Christ broke the authority that Satan had over us. He has provided a way for us to overcome the Devil. We must learn to apply our power based on who we are in Christ against the

Devil's attacks. Demons want to inhabit physical bodies because, through them, they can act out their vile sinfulness. A monster of lust cannot act out its evil unless it finds an individual willing to take part in acting out its desire. Evil spirits that attack the mind cannot enjoy tormenting someone unless they can entice them to join with them in processing wrong thoughts by igniting illicit passions.

The way a person can prevent hell from reigning in their life is through the proper appropriation of the life and work of Jesus Christ. Once a person has repented and confessed Jesus as Lord, demons cannot separate them from their eternal relationship with Jesus Christ. His sacrifice (based on His obedience) on the cross ended the control of hell over humanity. His resurrection put us in right standing with Father God. Now our bodies are free from sin's power, and hell cannot force us to live out its vileness. His shed blood cleansed us from the power of hell. We should make our minds and emotions available to the Holy Spirit for renewing, stopping the torment of hell's lies. God created our spirits to experience His divine presence, not to commune with darkness.

Because demons can possess unprotected people, we need to be careful not to join in alliance with someone who does not believe in Christianity's divine origin and authority. To do so could enslave us and confine us to common boundaries of thinking. The ruling influence of darkness in a person without restraint could pollute our liberty in Jesus Christ. It could hold us back from proceeding with God's plan for us. To think that darkness cannot mingle with light and pollute its virtue is not valid.

If the powers of light and darkness could not affect a Christian, God would not warn us not to "be unequally yoked" with those who deny that Jesus Christ is Lord. The stipulations an unprincipled life puts on a believer make it challenging to show oneself faithful to God's tasks.

Some believe that darkness and light cannot exist in an individual at the same time. A Christian's spirit is God's property paid for by the blood of Jesus, and an evil spirit cannot invade it. But to say that light and darkness cannot simultaneously dwell together is incorrect. If that were true, then Satan could not exist at all. God is omniscient, everywhere present in all places, all the time. Relegated to earth, Satan lives in the lower atmosphere. Eventually, he will occupy the darkest regions of hell. Hell is the absence of experiencing God. Satan's existence will ultimately be relegated to this realm. Currently, light and darkness can exist in the same place at the same time.

One of the most inadequate English translations in Scripture relates to the influence that demons have on human beings. The Greek term used by the Bible of those possessed by a devil is *daimonizomai*. The Greek word used for "demon" is *daimonion*. Why *daimonion* is accurately translated as demon, and *daimonizomai* was inaccurately translated as demon possession, and not merely being under the influence of a demon is a great mystery. *Daimonion* means "an evil spirit," and *daimonizomai* means "being under the power of an evil spirit." *Daimonion* is the agent; *daimonizomai* is the agent's activity. Hence, being demonized, a term our English Bible translators incorrectly translated as demon-possessed, is to be put under the power of an evil spirit to influence you. The level of this influence can be minimal, or the effect can be severe. However, ownership of the life of a Christian is not specified.

"Demon possession" is a term applied only to unbelievers. Webster defines it as "to occupy in person, to hold or have in one's keeping, to have and to hold, to have the legal title to, to have a just right to, to be master of, to own." Possession denotes ownership. Ownership implies controlling and holding onto something through legal occupancy. Ownership of a Christian's life is not an issue at all. God paid a great price to reconcile humanity. Demons can influence Christians but never possess them. Demonized, which means under the influence of, as a rendering for demon possession, is a better fit.

Demons can indwell people, but they can never take possession of a Christian. Demons do not legitimately "possess" anything of their own. Whatever they occupy, they get through trespassing. They invade people's lives by establishing a claim to areas of darkness in our lives. Demonization is a term that refers to influence. Demons can influence Christians, but they cannot own them. Webster defines the word "influence" as "the bringing about of an effect, physical or moral, by a gradual process." To the degree that you allow the enemy to influence you is the degree that demonization exists in your life. They will do anything we do not forbid them to do. They subtly change our behavior, so before we know it, we end up acting contrary to the law of God. The Bible is full of examples of people who "are demonized." There are no references to any of these people being Christians. So being totally under the control of a demon requires the Holy Spirit's absence. If the Holy Spirit dwells in a person's life, hell cannot completely control that person.

Demons affect people from all walks of life. Regardless of ethnicity or social status, demons can affect your life, trying to pour their vileness into you. They lie dormant, waiting for a condition suitable for their activity to arise, and then infiltrate our bodies with obstructions that affect our functioning towards our aims and goals. Various illnesses result from demon activity; many cause extreme pain and anguish, either in our body or mind. They love to disable our walk and weaken our faith through illness, causing intense distress and suffering. Still, Jesus came to heal and recharge our souls with spiritual authority, subduing the enemy, removing his influence, and making us whole, causing the attack of hell to pass away. He wants to restore what we lose and bring us back to God by replacing the curses of hell with the blessings of heaven.

God wants us to be free from the filth and vileness of demonic activity. Demons are filthy creatures that thrive on the forbidden. They want to infiltrate our lives with many failures. They want to cling to us and get involved in our conduct. However, they are powerless to stand against the authority of God. When confronted with the power of God, they cry like sniveling babies. They are spineless spirit beings that have no command of their own. They will try to sound great and give an appearance of power, but they are defenseless against a Christian who knows through experience that Jesus is Lord.

We can remove them and deprive them of power if we confront them with the lordship of Jesus Christ and the blood of the Lamb of God. They cannot resist or reject the authority of God. We must direct our attention away from hell and focus on the power of God. The force of God that hurled Satan to earth is the same force that a Christian will use to drive out demons today. At the feet of Jesus, we get the strength needed to stop these monsters from activating their powers against us.

When you encounter a demon, confront it with the lordship of Jesus Christ. The truth of the gospel breaks demonic influence. If you apply the power of God, as outlined in the Scriptures, against a demon, it must retreat. It cannot resist the persistence of a Christian who knows this. Regardless of the area a monster has occupied, it must let go when ordered to in the name of Jesus Christ. God is not a magical tool; you cannot carry Him around like a bag of tricks. For His power to drive out demons effectively, the agent dispelling the Devil must be in the right relationship with God. Knowable sin and areas of darkness in a person will prevent anointing. A devil is smart enough to know if you have compromised your sanctification. You cannot drive out a demon if you are not a clean vessel set aside for the Master's use. To be clean does not mean perfection. The level of light God reveals to us determines our accountability. The more we know, the more accountable we are. To walk in integrity before the Lord is living up to the revelation revealed to you.

There are many references in Scripture of people "being demon-ized." As stated, in all scriptural instances, the hosts are unbeliev-ers. The Lord healed all influenced by demons and restored them to their natural states. Of all the people brought to Jesus to receive ministry, not one example exists where He failed to heal and restore everyone. In every confrontation, Jesus cast out the demons. His authority would overcome the control of the Devil and deprived them of having power over their hosts. He expelled the demon and prevented it from returning. In Jesus Christ, we must remain active and healthy, not letting our resistance subside. Jesus prevents our destruction through His power's safety, preventing demons from having total control by removing their presence. With the influence of demonic activity coming from without instead of within, we can resist demonic attacks more effectively.

Satan wants to dull our senses and repress our keenness. He tries to remove our sensitivity to the things of God and dim our abilities. If he can minimize our capacity to receive from God, he can infect our lives. Jesus cleanses our physical bodies from satanic influence, allowing us to have the power of discernment. He gives us spiritual insight and the ability to get knowledge through our natural senses. God enables us to express our true natures.

Satan tries to deprive us of using our natural attributes, wanting to render us unable to fight against his attacks, but Jesus came to heal human lives. His visitation to earth brought health to our current physical circumstances. He has the power to straighten out our problems. God wants us to function with all of our capacity to live intact. He frees us from the deficiency of a broken and incomplete reality. We remove the deprivations of darkness by continually accessing the power of the cross. We must continue to find ourselves at the feet of Jesus because sudden assaults of hell disturb our serenity and make us apprehensive.

Fear takes our eyes off of Jesus and focuses them on our problems, making us dependent on our circumstances. We need to come to a place in life where we realize in Jesus, the total restoration of our nature is possible. We need to learn how to take advantage of God's authority and His saving power, which preserves us. To behold the power of God in our own lives is God's will for us. We are to put on the garments of God and curb our desires by exercising self-control. The events in life bring God's will to pass. The appearance of Jesus in history has forever changed the outcome of what we do. We no longer are under the curse of hell. We now realize that our inevitable good is the outcome of a Spirit-led life. The natural way to success is through understanding the working knowledge of God's power.

Learn to assimilate this working knowledge adequately so you can effectively ward off the enemy of your soul. A Spirit-filled Christian can resist the enemy on their behalf. If carefully and appropriately administered, it is possible to cast a demon out of your own life. That's right. Sometimes, self-deliverance is possible. However, it would be best if you were serious about any evil spirit encounter because this is a legal confrontation. You must have jurisdiction over the enemy to remove them from your life. It is imperative to know for sure, based on the blood of Jesus, you are in the proper relationship with God, as your life could depend on it. I believe that deliverance is a family business. Your spiritual brothers, sisters, mothers, and fathers need to understand that it is not abnormal to find oneself resisting an evil spirit in your life. They are everywhere and influence people daily. So for a Christian to need deliverance from darkness is not something weird or mystical. It is just like doing a little housecleaning.

Peeling layers of darkness off of your life is as natural as eating an artichoke. An artichoke has many layers on it. As you eat it, you peel layer after layer off until you get to the heart. Our lives get cluttered with stuff that just seems to pile up over the years. After you realize the enemy is the root cause of these problems, you cleanse and start peeling off layer after layer until finally, you have reached the heart of your dilemmas. God wants our hearts. He must peel layers of obstructions off of us to get to the center of our lives. The benefit of this process is the ability to stand in the presence of God with a heart purified by the Lord Jesus Christ.

Demons love to show off. Their arrogance is without measure. If we require an evil spirit to leave a person through a deliverance session, he will try to wreak havoc in his attempt to destroy on his way out. He does this through physical manifestations. His last act in a person's life is an attempt to compromise the person receiving healing's integrity like someone on social media that brags about something they did, only to get in trouble for posting their actions. On his way out, a demon will attempt to make a public show of his demise to manifest his disdain for the things of God.

Power is something that everybody in today's world is seeking. Satan knows this and offers the ability to influence others. He realizes people's desire for higher levels of awareness of life. The supernatural familiarity the Devil has with this world allows him to fabricate a person's ability to determine future events (Acts 16:16). Especially if people will use this awareness to control others, he counterfeits God's ways and provides an artificial ability to predict occurrences. Despite his lack of originality, Satan can still predict specific events because he has the power to make sure things come to pass. We must stop demons from having the right to govern our domestic affairs.

Our Authority Exercised

We have an advantage concerning the things of hell. The God who sees all things as if they were today and foretells future events accurately through the gift of prophecy has called us to Himself and invites us to call on His name. The authority over darkness belongs to Jesus, and God has given this authority to us of His own accord. He has committed to us His ability and has commissioned us to follow His lead in overpowering hell. In Jesus, we now can lawfully engage the power to require demons to submit and obey our commands. We can choose to let monsters stay or direct them to leave. Demons are subject to the rule of God, and we possess that authority in Jesus Christ. Satan doesn't worry if we preach the gospel. His actual fear of the believer lies in a believer's ability to find his proper authority in Jesus Christ. God has satisfied His legal requirement for humanity's sin by paying the price for it Himself, thus appeasing His wrath. He has cleansed us from the filth of our impure lifestyles. Like a gardener who removes weeds from his rose garden, God wants to prune away the useless things in our lives. Compelling darkness to depart using the force of God in Jesus Christ, we stop being conquered by the evil influences of this life that deprive us of power and learn how to conquer evil with good (Romans 12:21). You cannot defeat demons using the weapons of darkness. If you overcome problems in life using your efforts, then victory is carnal. The Holy Spirit gives life; the flesh produces death. If you fight demons in the flesh, you will lose. You must learn to overcome darkness with light. Jesus defeated Satan by not taking part in any of hell's ways. You cannot defeat evil by using its principles. You overcome darkness using the directives outlined in the Word of God. God's Word has given us everything we need to understand how to resist every attack of hell.

Everything that demons have taken from us is restorable. As commissioners who attend to the details of heaven, we are to take part in increasing the boundaries of the kingdom of God. Victory is ours. Like being arraigned in the courthouse of heaven and being found not guilty, Jesus has conquered hell. We ought to live in victory over darkness. The evil that comes upon us, based on our misdeeds, deprives us of the good God has intended for us. God wants us to be successful, fit, and useful for the Master's tasks, fulfilling our destiny and inheritance in Christ. God's will for us is spiritual prosperity.

Nothing in God's economy is common. There is a high value placed on all the things of God. To partake of the things of darkness diminishes the importance of God's economy. It also develops an arena for the fruits of the night to grow and develop. Who we are and what we do originates from that which we believe. We will always live according to what we hold to be true. Demons want to affect our belief system. They want to work out their evil plans against us by causing us to act like the world, resulting in a loss of genuine prosperity. If we become employed with this life's undertakings, we can miss God's call on our life. To obscure our call's divine duty by associating with barren activity cultivates a willingness to subdue the workings of God. Light overwhelms darkness and refutes any claim hell might find fault within this life of ours. Ignorance is dangerous. Knowledge is light, and ignorance is a lack of knowledge. Darkness requires some ignorance to operate. And the dark enables hell. We must shed light on the dark areas of our life.

The power of this light comes from our relationship with Jesus, who sits far above all principalities and powers. Because of this relationship, we are coheirs with Christ. From the vantage point of our godly inheritance, we operate in Christ's authoritative power here on earth. We use this authority to stop demonic activity from working in our lives through the Word of God. Through humble living, prayer, and confession of our failures, we can keep the Devil at bay.

Recognize this principle: The Devil can legally gain access to your life if he encounters anything like himself in it. When the Devil comes, if he discovers anything, such as resentment, hatred, bitterness, jealousy, rebellion, that he can identify with, he will exploit that area. Unless we repent when confronted with areas the Devil has overtaken, he will eventually control more sites. But if through submission to God we resist the Devil, God will put hell to flight. In any battle, the more you learn about your opponent gives you the best viable opportunity to defeat him. Learn to know your enemy. This knowledge must come from the Word of God.

CHAPTER 7:

WEAPONS OF WAR

Our Legal Rights

God picked you and me (John 15:16). He delights in us (Isaiah 42:1) and fights for us (Luke 18:7). Through His mercy, He has chosen us for such a significant time as this to receive preference unto salvation. But there remains that which we will receive an eternal dwelling. A setting apart from the things of this life, a realizing of who we are. God Himself came down to earth to establish the surety of this calling for every believer. God knew you before He formed you (Romans 8:29). You were a reality in God's mind designated beforehand to experience God's supreme love through purification before you physically came into being. God's operation in removing that, which is foreign to our reconciliation back to Father God, originated in Him. God removes that which defiles and pollutes our walk through the agency of His divine Spirit—we are to listen to the leading of God's Spirit when He speaks, yielding and obeying. As we walk the Christian life, we learn to comply with God's Spirit to have the authority needed to maintain a right standing before our heavenly Father. Divine life springs forth because of the saving grace of Jesus, the anointed One who shed His blood on our behalf. From beginning to end, it is all God. We contribute nothing but to yield and obey because God is the all-sufficiency of life, the sustainer of our walk.

We produce fruit in our yielded lives because of the power of the blood of Jesus. The impact Jesus had on humanity is indescribable. Depicting how much God loves us is a challenging task. We can but receive His unmerited favor and come to understand the vastness of His beauty through personal encounters. We see but a glimmer of His greatness calling us to obey as His will for us becomes more transparent and more apparent. God calls and empowers us. We are but to listen and act.

Fear in our lives grows out of an absence of the knowledge of God. The more we realize who we are in Christ and the provision God has set forth on our behalf, the more we can overcome any fear the enemy might try to throw our way.

The Word of God

When a person gives their word about something, it is a proclamation of a promise, a solemn oath supported with integrity. No one can take your word away from you; it is something you must choose to surrender. For your word to fail, it must falter because of an act of volition. Failure to uphold a promise is the only way to compromise a person's word. God has given us His word. His written Word breathes forth countless promises and perceptions of God. God's Word is proven (Psalm 18:30) (Proverbs 30:5). It is eternal (Matthew 24:35, Mark 13:31, Luke 21:33), irrevocable (Isaiah 55:11), is the truth expressed (Psalm 33:4), and brings healing (Psalm 107:20). His written oath to man (Psalm 105:8) portrays God's character and attributes, giving life direction (Psalm 119:105). God's Word is integrity established given to man by choice. It cannot falter in any of its content because that would require an act of volition by God. God can choose, but He cannot choose contrary to His Word because of who God is. He cannot select incorrectly or unintelligently because of His nature, which establishes His Word in heaven (Psalm 119:89) and is the earth's foundation.

The Word of God should be the foundation of our learning relative to the evil one. We should not use our discourses with darkness or our experiences with the enemy to determine our understanding. Everything we know about good and evil should reference the Word of God and the work of Jesus Christ. By establishing our identity on the Word of God, we solidify our stance against the enemy.

His Word gives us life (James 1:18) (1 John 1:1) (Philippians 2:16), saving us by becoming a part of us (James 1:21) (1 John 2:14), commissioning us to act (James 1:23). As the infinite message of God (1 Peter 1:25) (1 Thessalonians 2:13), it does not decay (1 Peter 1:23). Helping us grow (1 Peter 2:2) it reveals the power that sustains life (2 Peter 3:5, 7). It trips up the unbeliever (1 Peter 2:8) and is free from falsehood (1 John 1:10) (2 Corinthians 6:7) as it perfects us in love (1 John 2:5). Existing from the beginning (John 1:1) (1 John 2:7), it continues to grow (Acts 6:7, 12:24, 19:20) (2 Timothy 2:9). Hearing the Word enables the Holy Spirit (Acts 10:44) (Ephesians 1:13). It is available to everyone (Acts 15:7), building us up and giving us an inheritance (Acts 20:32). It is the sufficient promises of God (Romans 9:6,9) enabling faith (Romans 10:17), restoring harmony as it renews our friendship with God (2 Corinthians 5:19).

It was the agency of His creative powers (Proverbs 8:22-31).

Everything in the heavens and on the earth came into existence through God's Word (Colossians 1:16) (Psalm 33:6). God's Word supports and sustains all that exists (Hebrews 1:3). We can take a stand against the gates of hell based on the Word of God. It has placed us in a fixed and permanent position before Father God and is the Christian walk's stability (Psalm 119:101). With God at the beginning (John 1:1), it strengthens us (Psalm 119:28) and contains the essence of life (Psalm 119:50). God's Word allows us to experience the calm, undisturbed condition of the presence of God. The secrets of God's eternal presence revealed through the Word of God are authority enacted. God's Word articulates His ideas, thus making Himself known to man. The Word of God directs our paths. Because it's the principal authority of our work, it inspires and guides us (Psalm 119:9). It is the rule that guides us into the specific purposes of God. The Word of God persuades us concerning God's favor by inducing us to act, listen, and comply with the pure Spirit's leading, draws us to God, enabling us to determine the all-sufficient power of God (Romans 10:17). It is the guarantee of God's specific promises furnishing the benefits and privileges of God to man, helping us know and understand God, allowing us to overpower and overcome (Psalm 119:133, 170). It is the instrument to determine God's causes in debates, disputes, and controversies; the Word is the truth of God revealed.

It helps us to wait on God in expectation (Psalm 62:5). By learning the Word, we can prevent deception (Psalm 119:11). Satan misrepresents God's Word. Through untrue declarations, he tries to advance his position. However, through the servanthood of Jesus,

God's Word obligates divine service to humankind. It is the qualities of God perpetually engaged. Scripture declares God has put Himself in the place of a sinful man and has transposed humanity's sinfulness with the righteousness of Jesus Christ. It also states that God cannot lie (Titus 1:2) (Hebrews 6:18); therefore, God's expressed thoughts in His Word cannot declare false information. Deception is foreign to the thoughts and actions of God. Satan is always trying to make the lie seem like the truth. With God, it is impossible to utter anything other than fact (Psalm 119:160a). God's nature is unalterable; it cannot change (Hebrews 13:8). God cannot mislead you and will not disappoint you. God put Satan in his place by carrying our sins to the cross. He set forth the workings of His actions in the discourses of His written Word. Regarding its position, God has exalted His Word above His name (Psalm 138:2).

Demons have an intense desire to cause trouble or pain. They want to make us poor in spirit and exert their strength against us, causing us to become fatigued. They want to separate us from the ways of God and to distance us from God with the care of this temporal life. Even though they conceal themselves, they will respond to your requests. It is crucial when confronting demons always to have a posture supported by God's Word. They are aware of those who oppose their actions. The principles of God's Word give your life identity. Demons know if your life lines up with Scripture and if you are in right standing before God. If you oppose them without being adequately positioned in Christ, the result could damage (Acts 19:15, 16). We must be able to let them know who we are in Jesus Christ.

Our God-given authority applied in our lives based on the Scriptures' truth lets hell know that we are a force with power. If you are not living correctly and do not rightly divide the Word in your life, the enemy will not acknowledge your authority. The procession of our actions must stem from God's Word. Scriptural principles must be the origin of our efforts. Who we are in Christ should lead to restful results implemented by constructively applying the influence of God's indwelling presence. God should inhabit our conduct, as outlined in His Word. The abiding presence of God almighty exists in us; the One who calls eternity His home lives inside of us (Isaiah 57:15).

God's Word brings life to our lifestyle. It refreshes us and makes us strong. True to the radiant nature of God almighty is the appearance of action grounded in God's Word. His Word restores us. It is continually bringing us back from dead works to life by infusing us with vigor and courage. It renews our inner thoughts and gives life to our spirits and brings physical healing and cleansing. God reveals His saving grace in His written Word. His Word furnishes us with documentation about the fullness of God, enabling us to accomplish that which enriches others. God's Word allows us to abound with the virtues that lead to everlasting possessions. It makes us wise beyond our years. It enables us to form the best probable course for our lives and is the means to execute those plans, as it increases our capacity for spiritual understanding.

God's Word sets us apart for the tasks of heaven. God's renewing process outlined in His Word purifies our souls and frees our conduct from guilt. Living, according to God's Word, leads to holy living. It communicates the sacred priesthood of God, cleansing us of sensuality, and excites our senses to live in heavenly and modest purity. It teaches us to love the truth, speak the truth (Zech. 8:16), and live truthfully (John 3:21) before God and man. The facts and the reality of God's efficiencies are in His written Word.

God's Word is full of life and actively employs God's interactions with man. It cuts right to the chase of a matter, considering all angles, equipping you to engage in hand-to-hand combat with the forces of hell. It can help you work through any problem you encounter. By channeling our actions through God's Word, we can establish grounds by which to live. Enduring any challenge thrown against it, it reveals the intimacies of God. It penetrates the darkness and shows us the way into the inner actions of God. If we understand the Word of God supports us, we can boldly force our way into enemy territory. It distinguishes the genuine from the counterfeit. God's Word etches out our lot in life, revealing the true destiny of humankind, and is a fundamental component of the whole of God, constituting His determinations. It separates the dead work from that which is alive, and it enables us to war against that which seeks to destroy the essence of life, eliminating the undue claims of the ungodly to live apart from God. It helps us develop the will of God that allows us to rule and govern life's affairs approved by God and to reflect upon life's experiences with God's maturation. God's Word penetrates the affections of man.

The Word of God is the way of life, and it breeds faith unto salvation. By taking residence in us, it frees us from judgment, bringing life as its fruit. It commissions us to believe in the person and function of Jesus Christ (John 3:36) and reveals the will of Father God for us (John 6:40). We escape the pollution of the world by abiding in the Word of God.

Trust in God's Word guards the center of our lives. It establishes a fence of defense to block the attacks of the evil one. By silencing the accusations of hell, it applies the seal of God to our actions. The Word of God confirms the authenticity of our deeds. God's Word conveys the privilege of professing the power of God as being voluntarily engaged on our behalf. We ground this power in the working out of the Word of God through the Holy Spirit.

We are to render ourselves as instruments of God through acknowledgment of His Word. Purified of every fault, we are worthy of the honor and respect that Jesus Himself deserves. God's Word proclaims us positionally perfect in Christ Jesus. It places us at the highest care and reverence available to His creation. Purified by salvation, it presses us into action as His Word declares us free from the corrupt desire of sin, cleansing us of the guilt associated with lewd conduct. The Word of God establishes a shield of truth around us. As we live undefiled from the things of this life, the Word of God declares us clean, without stain or blemish, through supernatural bathing. It cleanses the death of our sinfulness in the bath of the Word of God. Like fountains of pure spring mountain water, the breath of God refreshes us. He pours His life into us through the meditation on His Word. God's Word is the instrument of attack against the onslaught of hell. Confronting Satan and his minions by the proper implementation of the Word of God defeats them. The Word of God engages God's authority on our behalf.

God wants us to hang on every word He breathes forth. He wants us to heed His Word and apply it. By observing what comprises the Word of God, we learn how to keep ourselves in check. The embodiment of this life, what He (God) intends to do, His exhortations, advice, commands, and direct communication to humanity, is His written Word.

The Scriptures convey the foundation of our expectation of a future dwelling place with God. The same way you put something you intend to buy online in a cart, God has reserved a place for us in heaven.

You get success on the path of life through the constant pursuit of Christ. A way traveled on daily becomes well worn and develops familiar markings, making it easy to follow. If trouble or distress comes, the standard markings on the path give you confidence that you are moving in the right direction. We prosper in God by taking the Holy Spirit by the hand and receiving His access to the path of God. The Holy Spirit gives us joy in degrees that surpass any conflict we might encounter along the way.

God's inward work through the Word can work in you through an outworking of power. It puts forth the power of God and is obtainable for practical application in everyday living. By placing confidence in God's powerful Word, it credits us with the capacity to stand against the forces of hell. The competence and sufficiency of God's resources in His written Word help us prevail over the things of this life. Its influence and inclinations are sufficient in presenting the motives of God. God is for us, and He will do anything He can to help us succeed. The evidence of God in His Word enables us to accept the testimony of Jesus as God's authority revealed to man. God has taken hold of man, and man can take hold of the hand of God. His Word is God's truth forever expressed to man. God has paid the price. Humanity has but to take God's gift provided as payment for our debt. We are to give admission to the events of God and accept His presence in our lives as our minds continue to grow in knowledge. The capacity to learn increases by washing our minds of this life's clutter through God's Word.

Surrendering our will through faith in Jesus allows us to communicate God's things and gives us a position of honor and respect deserving only to those of royal stature. The act of God in satisfying payment for the penalty of our sin has extinguished the required judicial discharge of our actions. The visitation of the Word of God removes the guilt and suffering of sin. God's Word reveals to us the possibility of possessing the condition of being holy and innocent. A state that allows us to conform to the Law of God.

Certain things that happen to us are not by chance. Whether sadness, failure, calamity, or mishap, it is all intended to strengthen our grip on the kingdom of God. Satan wants us to suffer and become weary. He desires to expose us to danger. He wants us to feel obliged to sin and engages his operatives to impose his will on us. God wants the things in this life to impress upon our minds the passion of His majesty. Even though trouble or distress afflicts our walk, God is obligated to the promises of His limitless Word. Not limited to this life's limitations are the unleashing of power and the release of God's mind. The constraint of this life does not confine the exercise of God's Word. It is boundless with the ability to expand the understanding of all who embrace its truth. The Word of God is the external instrument used for engraving God's internal impressions on the heart of man.

Jesus Himself is present in our lives. His existence causes things to happen. He separated Himself from Father God for such a time as this. Time being forever changed by the visitation of the living Word as God physically became a part of this temporal reality to enable His brightness to shine forth and beam upon this world. God's arrival in the person of Jesus Christ changed the point of contact between the temporal and the divine forever. It pleased God to announce His opinions and perspectives concerning people. To know God intimately is the most glorious and exalted state of consciousness possible. The work of Jesus has appointed a future hope as a present reality. God's Word is the groundwork that gives firmness to the validity of the existence of God. With confidence, we stand firm on Jesus, who is God revealed.

By placing ourselves under the authority of God's Word, we maintain our position in the presence of God. It sets things in their proper balance by measuring immovable truth with the forces of temporal reality. The Word of God is the support needed to keep you from falling. It is the force that raises the level of living above the ordinary standards of this life. Collectively, the Word of God impacts everything that exists. The foundation of life is the fountain of life. As the living Word of God, Jesus is able, by His elevated position, to perform the miracle of changing the ultimate resting place of every residing soul forever. Human impurities no longer separate man from God.

God Himself has blown open the gates of hell forever and set the distinction between that which results in eternal damnation and leads to life everlasting. He has done this in Himself; by ushering in His new world order, He authored the path of life to prepare for those who would heed His Word and turn to a saving knowledge of Jesus Christ. From His vantage point in the heavenly realm, Jesus upholds the word of His power as the foundation of everything that exists. We are seated with Him, forever settling the posture of believers in Christ. Just as God's Word is firm in heaven, so is the place of honor and authority of every Christian. The Word reveals the outpouring of God's significant influence over humanity.

God's motivation in providing His written Word is to increase our capacity for spiritual truth and give evidence to its author. The scriptural influence that persuades us to become acquainted with its message is faith. The essence of reality is the conviction that God is an actual being who loves and cares for what He created. God is the one with supreme authority over all that is real. Understanding and knowing this truth is the underlying theme of the Scriptures. The enduring influence of God is clear. He interacts with creation every moment of every day. It brings His reflections to completeness by those who fashion themselves according to His Word. God has remained invisible. To physically see God, we must see Him in creation. The evidence of God in the life of a Christian is the reflection of God's infinite being. Renewed man is God's power revealed. To live as one ought to is not perfect conduct. It merely recognizes the existence of God as we change our behavior in response to His written Word.

The occasion for trouble is constant. Knowing by experience that Christianity is a normal lifestyle is fundamental to success. Trials press in at every turn. Despite the influences that counter our walk with God, we must persist in our purpose in life. God's Word provides strength to resist discouragement, so we do not abandon our faith. A successful attempt to find out the quality of Christian living ends with endurance.

The mantle of God is Jesus revealed. He is the commander and ruler, the covering of God that equips us to success. He is the composition and essential part of success. The living thoughts of God expressed in the Word of God come to life.

Obedience to God's Word releases us from the shackles that prevent true freedom. Existential knowledge of the truth that sets you free is like the intimacy of a husband and wife's relationship. It is personal stimulation of the senses as they relate to God's supernatural intervention with His people. That intimate oneness with your mate that sends chills up and down your spine is a natural example of this phenomenal work. It is interacting with God in a way that changes the entire scope of your thought life. Your entire way of living is permanently changing to understand a new and fulfilling way of relating to life. The knowledge of the Scriptures reveals the factual element of this liberation.

We should speed up that which causes us to actuate fondness about the things of God. The price of honor given upon us because of the timeless sacrifice of Jesus far outweighs anything offered in today's economy. We should never whittle down the value of the ingredients of our salvation. Instead, we need to develop a proper understanding of God's Word so we can undertake God's work by employing an appropriate knowledge of the Scriptures. It requires effort on our part to accomplish the things God wants from us. The misappropriation of truth distorts the open position of a believer. Not communicating the truth of Scripture injures the reputation of a Christian. We must sharpen our skills to straighten out any improper perceptions of the message of God's Word. The clarity of God's original letter to man is pure and makes up the full measure of God's attributes and integrity. As messengers of God, we must apply ourselves to understand how to separate the various truths of Scripture to extract their true meanings. Satan's knowledge and misuse of Scripture can cause Christians who do not know the Scriptures to hinder God's work. When the prince of darkness confronted Him, Jesus rightly divided God's written Word as His only defense. The Word of God, when properly applied, stops hell dead in its tracks.

Obedience

Obedience is voluntarily engaged in an action, yielding your desire by surrendering its power to another. We have already determined that biblical obedience is not perfect living; it lets God steer you by guiding your life with His directives for living. It is complying with godly authority by subjecting our desires to the proper restraint of God's standards. Simply put, it is applying the principles as outlined in the Scriptures to our lives. We need to learn how to respond to God when He is knocking at the door of our lives. Like a doorman at a fancy establishment, we must immediately respond when God approaches and allow Him passage. We must understand the truth of His ways and know how to apply them to our lives so that we can reconcile ourselves back to the Father when we sin or disobey. True liberation is living dependent on the Lord by obediently exposing our sins when we fail Him; disobedience makes God a stranger to your ways.

Disobedience distances you from God and breeches your fellowship with Him. It causes God to withdraw from you because He cannot have a connection with sin. It also withholds a blessing. Rather than growing with an ongoing relationship with God, reflecting on past failures can cause you to become indifferent to God's things. The preciousness of His presence can become distant, opening you up to further waywardness, which can cause you to experience something avoidable. If we stray from the golden path, the fullness of God becomes an empty pathway. The void of complete separation from God is not realistic to a Christian. But if you disobey Him, you can experience a loss deep within your soul. You can feel empty, lonely, and abandoned. However, God has promised never to leave us or forsake us. Come to a point in life where you never leave or forsake the things of God. His presence is the sustaining force of this physical reality. It is also the sustaining force in the life of a Christian. To live a Christian life without the abiding presence of God is like trying to have a relationship with someone who is standing five miles away from you without the use of an electronic device. A Christian should always remain close to God in an intimate and obedient relationship.

However, when things do not go as they should, and we do sin, we must do whatever it takes to bring us back into a proper relationship with Father God. Choice can influence divine providence over the affairs of man. To prevent exposure to the wiles of the Devil, we need to maintain our walk by making proper decisions. If we choose incorrectly, it opens us up to unwarranted attacks and traumas. Obedience to the over six hundred commands of the law was not God's original intention. He knew it would be impossible for humankind to obey the letter of the law. Instead, its design was to identify sin. When we recognize sin in our lives and apply the principles of obedience, we can prevent undue assaults from the forces of hell.

Jesus distanced Himself from God on our behalf. Our disobedience caused Him to experience separation from the divine. Jesus experienced the pain of our spiritual death so we could have fellowship with God. He shared the rejection of God so that God would never again reject us. Obedience, in its purest sense, is the life of Jesus Christ. Just like our lungs do not spend energy and function unto themselves but operate unconsciously, breathing in life to our mortal bodies, we are to function according to the principles of Jesus and use our energies to live for others' wellbeing. We are to choose service over self-interest. The former existence, with its self-centered-ness, no longer determines the state of good living. The life of Jesus stirs us to produce actions that arouse the senses to wholesomeness and abundant life.

God has called us to listen to Him and yield our will by complying with His commands. He wants us to submit to His authority and allow Him to rule in our lives through the Scriptures' precepts because to disobey is resisting the power and control the Bible affords. It is not responding to God's guidance and, in stubborn defiance, choosing not to align our life up with the teachings of the Bible. Disobedience knows the law of God to be a higher authority and deliberately disregards its message. Disobedience prevents improvement, leaving the things of God undone, causing undue suffering. God wants us to devote our lives to the service of worship and to dedicate ourselves by setting aside our ambitions and presenting our consecrated lives as an offering of thanksgiving at the altar of His throne. He has forever atoned for our sin. We have but to surrender our self-will and live lives given over to divine order interests. To buy favor with God is not the issue. In Christ Jesus, we are forever perfect before Father God. Obedience is merely the sacrifice God deserves, and it requires living life set apart for God to fulfill all the determination of God for your life.

Sometimes in life, things happen we do not understand. You may work for a boss who is not fair, or you might have to put up with a relative who denies your faith or submit to the teachings of a teacher who hates God. Assure yourself God has an eternal purpose for your life. When tough times come, it is vital to seek God and find His purpose and the true meaning behind your circumstances. To defeat the darkness, Jesus realized He had to remain faithful to the call of God in His life. The ultimate call in His life was to stop Satan's plan through obedience. That call was more important to Jesus than overcoming the immediate obstacle in His life. When trouble surfaces, determine what God is doing and how you should respond. Know the cup that the Father has chosen that you should drink from and fulfill His will for your life. Successfully standing against the enemy's intents must include God's will for our lives. Sometimes our circumstances seem like they have the upper hand on us. So we turn our attention to changing them when some of those circumstances are necessary for us to accomplish all that God has for us ultimately. We might want to seek help from our friends when God has intended for us to walk through our troubles with Him. Our friends' good intentions can prevent God's purposes from coming to pass in our life. If we fight against hell without understanding God's plan for us, we might end up fighting the battle using the wrong weapons.

Like a dead person responding to being kicked is one ingredient to success in this life for the Christian. To keep any part of our former life alive makes it easier to stumble on our walk with God. Jesus crucified the avenues of sin in our mortal bodies. When He hung on the cross, He took with Him everything in us that caused us to cling to the old way of living. We were on the wrong side of the cross. Dead in sin. Jesus went beyond man's sinfulness to the farthest side of darkness and made a public spectacle of purgatory itself. Our old life sold us into slavery by sin, totally under the control of its evil vices, indulging its deadly tentacles without the ability to free ourselves from its snare. Allowing its power to draw us away, we were living as enemies of God.

But God showed us His great love in that even when we were His enemies willfully denying Him, Jesus bridged the gap through His great love for us. He led the Love of God through His obedience. We must not let the things that can destroy us govern our lives by cleansing our conduct to bear fruit fit for the Master's use. In genuine sincerity freeing ourselves from the corrupt desire of sinful behavior, which leaves guilt in its wake, we are not to indulge the evil passions and appetites that sever the stability of our Christian walk. To openly abandon the things of God breaks down the protective barrier established by pious conduct.

It is important to remember that what we do affects our emotions. The sentiments we experience are direct ramifications of our actions. That's why God says that obeying is better than any sacrificial offering. It shows we have control over our inner passions. We are not to live by our feelings, as our natural senses can negatively affect how we live. Ever since sin entered the mind of man, forbidden desire has inflamed human passions with an eagerness to adorn us with that which is not lawful. Sin limits our fulfillment and prevents us from possessing the peace that passes all understanding. It is necessary to deprive the power of our sinfulness that destroys our testimony in Jesus by using His strength to defeat our carnal desires by identifying with His death.

Through the working out of our salvation, we can live in resurrection power. It is important to rid ourselves of improper conduct.

When we become entangled in sin, it is by choice. Liberation from sin is also through personal selection. When we engage our actions, we choose obedience, leading to salvation, or disobedience, leading to corruption. It is that simple; we choose to live right with God or choose to disobey God. Called to action, we are to depart from sin and break our union with the corruption whose deeds of darkness destroy our fellowship. We should no longer carry our sins' mantle. By laying aside our sinful propensities, we construct a lifestyle that establishes obedience as its foundation. Every individual has a natural disposition to sin. The roots of these impulses lay in a fallen nature that is always trying to lead you astray. Like a fish lured up with bait, this sinful nature causes desires to rise to the surface and entangle us in the web of deceit, leading to inappropriate conduct.

If neglected, sin multiplies like a mole allowed to construct as many molehills as it desires to create an excellent underground passageway. Left unfettered, the paths to these many hills of sin soon become mountains of misdeeds. For this to happen, we must long for sin. We must stretch out and try to grasp it and choose to give ourselves over to its mastery. To control our lives, sin will strut its stuff like a rooster in a henhouse trying to wrap you up with its arrogant lifestyle. Like a pot of boiling water, we will overflow with vile action if we do not douse the flame that fans its impropriety. The reproach of sin causes injury. It gives an evil declaration whenever it's enabled dishonoring and disfigures our walk with God. When Jesus died on the cross, sin nature died a horrible death—forever separated from God. We live in the right relationship with God because of our choice to follow Jesus.

We are to remove by force from our minds anything that denies the evidence of Scripture stating that Jesus Christ is God. It is imperative that you take whatever denies the proof of Christ's Deity captive and strenuously displace it from your consciousness. Not by physical force but by an inner strength manifesting through stable thought processes that enable conduct that defeats darkness. Without ceasing, hell is throwing flaming arrows at our minds. Learn to identify the thoughts of anguish so you can remove them. Our gaze should never steer from God's plan for us. Like casting a legal vote for a political candidate, we should choose to perform the mandates of heaven. Satan created the realm of darkness by trying to exalt himself above the stars of God (Isaiah 14:13). Righteousness exalts (Proverbs 14:34). Humility exalts (Luke 14:11). But when we choose to elevate ourselves, we reduce God's dignity and power to the levels of darkness. God has revealed the truthful facts, which, when applied, result in exaltation. We are to coordinate our minds and bring them under God's control by imprisoning thoughts that oppose His divine Word. No servant is more significant than his master. Obedience to Christ is the duty of all who belong to the family of God.

God's divine order begins in our minds. A natural by-product of subjecting yourself to God makes Satan your opponent because he actively hates and opposes all followers of Jesus. However, when you yield the throne of your life to Jesus Christ, you establish the substance needed to resist hell's demonic forces. Because of the change that has occurred in your life, you can prevent Satan from influencing you. If you act on your faith, you can render his purposes incapable of poisoning your life. By counteracting his motives with God's plan for your life, you can stop Satan dead in his tracks by standing on the ground of the cross. Stand up against the powers of darkness, just like you would stand up to someone who tried to take something of yours that didn't belong to them. Proper identification with Jesus Christ gives a person the ability to put Satan to flight. Darkness will run from you, and hell's demons will hasten off in a cowardly fashion if you correctly implement the power of the cross.

Humility Cures Worldliness

God commands moderation in the indulgence of natural appetites. It is necessary to maintain attentiveness and alertness in discovering and avoiding evil. For God to provide safety free from the demonic arousals of this life, we need to conduct ourselves piously. Learn not to throw off the safety of obedient action and avoid conduct that causes the demonic activity to function freely without restraint. Satan is always looking to consume and destroy. His appetite for evil is ravenous, and his goal is the destruction of the human species. Like a punch in the gut, his minions want to knock the wind out of us. But a life firmly fixed on the promises of God establishes God's abiding presence as a protective shield that stops Satan's attacks.

A boxing match pits two fighters who are attempting to defeat each other using offensive and defensive tactics. When one boxer is punching, the other boxer is trying to fend off his blows. When the fighter on the offensive stops pursuing his opponent, the defensive boxer takes the offensive and punches. Both boxers are always trying to gain an advantage over their opponent. Similarly, when we stop resisting hell in our lives in the spiritual realm, the enemy looks to take another punch at us. We must make sure that we keep ourselves well protected by continuously maintaining an offensive posture.

Obedience and love are two garments every Christian should wear, as they distinguish the true believer from those who have a presupposition to temporal dispositions. The purity emitted from a Christian's life based on an internal supply of divine energy resulting in holy conduct is a divine revelation made manifest. How we conduct ourselves brings forth what we truly believe as it exposes our inner motives and is evidence of that which we base our lives on. It is apparent for all to see, not what we want others to suppose of ourselves. Conduct differentiates the believer from the unbeliever. However, grace saves us, not works. What we do can never make us acceptable to God because our acceptance is in the finished work of Jesus. He is the tangible expression of God's approval to all who believe. However, the way we conduct ourselves is evidence of the effects of the life-changing grace of God.

Because of grace, there should be no question or doubt in the minds of any we encounter relative to the foundational basis of our lives. Jesus Christ working in us should produce the fruit of righteous conduct in our everyday affairs. Proper moral behavior is merely acting by design. As Christians, we are under obligation to function according to His (God's) structure. He is the rightful owner of our lives. As members of the family of God, right living and unconditional love are natural attributes. He has deposited into our account all that belongs to Him. Though His characteristics limit Him from doing anything unwise, He renders help in life. That is why it is vital to conduct ourselves appropriately by expressing reverence to God in the things we do. Improper conduct based on wrong choices limits the hand of God (Psalm 78:41).

There is an intense desire to cover up our actions when we fall short of what we know God wants us to do. However, when we make a mistake, these extreme measures to prevent exposure can sacrifice the wellbeing of those dear to us. It is possible to think that the only way we can win is if someone else loses. As this is one reason, we should never compare our deeds with those of another. God has enough blessings for the entire world. No one can rob you of your blessing except yourself. Nothing outside of yourself can prevent God's will for your life. Never should we attempt to gain favor with God or man at the expense of another. To do so causes pain and agitation. It expresses the labors of hell itself.

If you are a Christian, then by biblical definition, God is your Father. Because the blood of Jesus now flows through your veins, you have entered a new existence. As designed, you can now live above the influence, corruption, and decay of your old fallen nature. You share in the stock of God himself and can now attend to the affairs of heaven. By choice, you keep yourself in a state of right standing by observing the essential things of God. You learn to know what is real and reject what is false.

When Jesus appeared in human history, He learned through experience what it meant to be a finite being by limiting His capacity as the personal and infinite Creator of the universe. Jesus conformed to the ways of being human. He adhered to the customs of a natural man. To behold Him in His humanness was to see a normal man abiding by the conditions of humanity. He walked on this earth with both feet firmly planted in the low state of a temporal lifestyle. By His own choice, He clothed himself with the garment of this often insufficient earthly existence. He knew the call of Father God in His life and stayed the course. Being free from the pride that unites itself with contempt for others, He understood meek and lowly living. His example enables the Christian to maintain a modest view of one's self. When we realize that we have allowed lofty things to enter our life, we should humble ourselves (1 Peter 5:6). Self-dependence establishes a barrier that prevents God's intervention in our lives.

Jesus was infinite in understanding. However, becoming human allowed Him to see firsthand the limitations of finite man. His obedience to the will of the Father (even though He eternally coexisted with Father God before time began) to go to the cross is the most excellent example of the love God has for humans. Jesus not only died for us; we murdered Him. It was not Satan or any of his demons that killed Jesus. It was the sin of humankind that caused the Son of glory to experience the disgrace of the cross. When Jesus walked the earth, crucifixion was the most shameful, dishonorable method of punishment used by man, reserved for the basest of criminals. It was the lowest form of public humiliation a person could undergo and was the type of death that sin deserved. When Christ died for our sins, He made a stand on behalf of all humankind. In plain view,

He remained intact without wavering from the purpose of His human existence. He upheld God's power and sustained the Highest's authority, thus establishing once and for all His kingdom's authority. By forcing upon Himself the guilt of the entire world, He became the immovable foundation, paving the way for the saints of God to continue in His steps, safe from the threat of perdition.

Jesus is the only begotten of the living God. He is Yahweh incarnate. The face of God Himself revealed to man. Yet, He suffered from weakness and experienced the mortality of humankind. Using His natural faculties, He increased in the knowledge of what it meant to be obedient to God's purpose in this life. In doing so, He furnished the example of living that we are to pattern ourselves after. Jesus was not ashamed to associate Himself with the lowest caste of people. He is no respecter of persons. To Him, all people are equal and deserve the highest rank of His sonship. God is the Father of all, and Jesus is the Savior of the entire world. By dying for the sins of His murderers, Jesus made clear the value He places on humanity.

As Christians, we should appraise the things we learn about this value we carry and become accustomed to the force of the Holy Spirit as He directs us to our ultimate aim. That aim is obedience to the will of God. By complying with heaven's affairs, we can observe the divine protection of His limitations on the call God places on us. This call harkens us to listen to the Holy One when He knocks on the door of our life and to comply. We walk in liberty, but God has placed on us the requirements of submissive living. Don't let the experiences of the fallen life affect the way you respond to God. His will for us does not guarantee that we will not suffer. However, His sacrifice eternally deposited the pledge of God on our behalf. We reap His benefits in this life because we have obeyed the call of God. We jeopardize the safety of this temporal protection every time we do not conduct ourselves properly. God changes us daily. He draws us to Him with every set of circumstances that occur. Even though His blessings are often contingent upon obedience, in Christ Jesus, we have an eternal purpose. Because of this, it is not possible to nullify His sacrifice for our sins every time we fail.

Gifts of the Holy Spirit

It is because we fail Jesus died. Remember obedience is not sinlessness (Jesus was the only sinless person). It is doing the things required to re-establish your relationship with God when you fail. Gifts resulting from the Holy Spirit's particular operation, like speaking with a heavenly language, casting out devils, and healing, are (Mark 16:17, 18) often communicated by the laying on by mature believers' hands (Acts 8:17, 19:6, 1 Timothy 4:14). These divine gifts are still active in the church today.

A gift is something you gain without exerting your action, with no influence from the recipient. The contributions of the Holy Spirit are the transference of divine force. God sent His Son so the Holy Spirit could clothe us with His supernatural influence. The gift of salvation is full payment equal to the required exchange of the penalties for the entire human race's sins. God compensated for our sinfulness by conferring our actions' liability to a yielded Savior who furnished payment in full. Jesus accepted the challenge and publicly gave up His preeminence by resigning Himself to the cross' abandonment. God's gift of eternal salvation thus became a reality. Man failed; Jesus yielded, breaking hell's force forever.

Now, this newness of life is available, supported by the Holy Spirit's equipping, who gives upon us His free and unmerited gifts. However, these gifts are not without a price. Father God can't share His glory with man. It is equally impossible for Jesus to share His glory with fellow man. So it should not come as a surprise that Holy Spirit cannot share His glory either. Today, many Christians are trying to figure out God's will for their lives, not realizing that they are preventing God's very influence revealed through the Holy Spirit from participating in their everyday activities. Christians should abandon the past paradigms and become accountable to God by crediting the Holy Spirit's influence. We should adopt a yielded posture, so the power of the Holy Spirit can reveal to us the very nature of God. To walk in the fullness of God is to remove ourselves from the throne of our lives and allow God's Holy Spirit to rule and reign from within. The Holy Spirit of God is, in fact, a gift from the Father (Acts 2:38). You cannot purchase divine gifts (Acts 8:20). A follower of Jesus receives them freely (Acts 10:45). Acceptance before God is a gift based on Christ's actions (Romans 5:18; 6:23).

God's nature is love. From which stems all of His other attributes. Love is the essence of influence that makes the gifts of God effective. These gifts are specific to each individual (1 Corinthians 7:7). We are not to neglect God's blessings (1 Timothy 4:14). Like starting a campfire, fan the flame of spiritual gifts into maturity (2

Timothy 1:6). Everything received that is good is a gift from God (James 1:17). The Holy Spirit pours His skills upon us so that others might profit from them (Philippians 4:17), producing the effects designed to draw people to the Lord. God will always certify the Holy Spirit's work by supporting the truth with tangible evidence, not just mere words.

The stamp of approval that seals the gifts of God is the testimony of God Himself. He authenticates His contributions by visibly enabling individuals to see the truth of His actions. Our senses furnish evidence of the existence of solid, liquid, gas, animal, vegetable, or mineral. Similarly, God's actions declare to the human mind that His Spirit is actively working in the invisible realm that is among us. The spreading of the gospel is, to the greatest extent, a working of the extraordinary gifting of the Holy Spirit. God supernaturally plants His truth into men's lives through Christians who allow the Holy Spirit's gifts to work in and through them. The Holy Spirit's skills vary in external appearance. Yet, they are all derived from the same source. A genuine miracle is the supernatural strength and power of God revealed. The ability of a Christian stems from the virtue of God's very nature. The gifts of the Spirit are the resources of God. It is a beautiful thing to see the Holy Spirit at work. God distributes His gifts by actually giving us the right to function supernaturally and extraordinarily. It is a natural function of a follower of Jesus to live according to the Holy Spirit's gifts' workings. Not doing so is neither ordinary nor natural in the eyes of God. God Himself wills us to embrace His skills concerning the value of their operations through the exercise of our submitted wills, not our self-centered desires.

God wants us to become people who actively use spiritual gifts that have caused us to travel beyond our natural limitations. Developing an understanding of the divine Spirit's actions moves you to the right side of the cross. This enablement is not without trial and error; it takes time to develop your gifting. Mistakes do not show you are on the wrong path. It is merely traveling a trail that starts with the unknown; as you use your gifts, you understand how they work. Accustomed to living by natural means, most of the church will not accept the whole concept of spiritual gifts. Instead, their lives are void of the power that distinguishes them from the rest of humanity.

Satan leads the church away from spiritual gifts by making them seem weird and unconventional. Keeping Christians from tapping into the force of eternity, Satan gets Christians to bow to idols of tradition and dead works, unable to communicate genuine truth. Whatever represents the form of godliness, short of stepping out in true faith, is abnormal. God does not prefer us to live like this. God wants us to seize His gifts and to press in and take hold of our spiritual inheritance. To arrive at our destination in this life, we must follow the guiding light of God and clasp unto the force and influence of the Holy Spirit. If you get hooked by experiencing your spiritual gifts, you will wrap your arms around God in a way you never dreamed possible. I know some people will think that this part of Bible teaching is not for them, but I propose to you that God has called every Christian to develop their spiritual gifting. If you call Jesus Lord, then God wants to see your gifts in action. It is impossible to declare that Jesus is Lord of your life without the Holy Spirit's influence (1 Corinthians 12:3). The only way to have a thorough knowledge of God is to experience everything He has for you. Jesus has laid up for every Christian specific gifting. We should seek to make these talents obvious by functioning in them in plain view. Again, the distribution of these gifts differs from one another. They have different physical signs, yet they are common in their origin. To have a common goal, you must have a common control.

The Holy Spirit is the author of all functioning outward Godly manifestations. He is the central theme behind everything that God is doing in the world. To deny this makes for uncommon ground. It creates the gap the enemy of our soul needs to keep us wanting the strength of God. If we are feeble, we can only be a facsimile of the reality of God in our lives. We cannot function in the capacity needed to convince a dying world that Jesus is Lord without the Holy Spirit.

Of course, there are different services in the body of Christ. Each with their affections. But we are all executing the commands of the same God. We are all servants of the same King. We should eagerly seek to embrace our God's endeavors like a messenger sent to deliver a message that would change the course of battle in a major war. Like gallant warriors of the cross, we are at war. We should not be fearful and wanting of courage in the execution of God in our lives. Wake up, bride of Christ. God is for us. He is crying out to help a dying generation, not preparing traps along the way to trip us up. He is waiting for us to take up the trumpet of His call so we can make deposits into our heavenly bank account. It is God Himself who promotes in us the ability to function according to His purpose for us. We belong to God. The effectiveness of our gifts is His responsibility. We are merely to operate in them and let the working of God reach others with His Spirit's influence.

Our life is a constituent part of a whole, a measure assigned to us as we seek our place in life. We all have various gifts given to us by the Creator. All of which allows us to bear one another's burdens. Our gifting brings us together. We urge each other along by making ourselves suitable for the tasks of life. Our gifts make us profitable. It is imperative that we openly use our skills that others might benefit from them. God has furnished us with the tools. It is up to us to use them and develop an acute awareness of the broad knowledge available to us in discovering the prudent use of God's gifts. The formation of our skill and craft in your spiritual gift develops as we execute the councils of God. The deeper our relationship with God, the larger our gifting becomes. Remember it is the same divine Spirit that imparts to us all our lot in life. The wise one, the knowledgeable one, the one of great faith, the healer, the miracle worker, the prophet, the deliverer from the darkness all derive their talents from the same source. As the Holy Spirit wills, He makes us valuable. This usefulness is divine and structured according to our natural talents. We are to be ourselves, not something we're not. As we find our true identities in Christ, the Holy Spirit fashions us through the equipping of His gifting.

The Cross

The message of the cross is not sacrificing but obedience. Jesus died the death of a criminal. He did this not because He was guilty but because we were guilty. If we received the condemnation we deserved, we would experience crucifixion's grievous punishment throughout all of eternity. Jesus suffered the guiltiest death possible to keep sinners from the eternal damnation of being forever tormented and separated from God. Ceasing to exist would be a far greater outcome than to live eternally separated from the goodness of God, for hell in its most basic form is total separation from God's goodness. Everything good comes from God. Hell is the absence of everything good. The Bible says that all have sinned and fallen short of God's glory (Romans 3:23). Though every human being deserves to go to hell, God made a plan of escape for humanity. He did this by penetrating the halls of time and paying the price Himself. Jesus existed before time began in fellowship with the Father and the Holy Spirit in timeless infinity. He entered His finite creation and made it possible for us to become reunited with God according to our original design.

The cross of Jesus Christ changed the entire course of history, which is, again, His story. Since the beginning of time, creation has been waiting in expectation for the Savior of the world. His birth changed the method of dating time itself. With His death and resurrection, God ushered in the restoration of man to Himself. The eternal destiny of every individual pivots on which side of the cross one lives. One must lay down his life to receive the divine life made available through the cross of Jesus Christ, which is a daily act and is a requirement for all faithful followers of Jesus. To learn from Jesus Himself, we must deny our self-agendas and be ready to become obedient to Scripture's teaching. The message of the gospel is folly to man's intellect. Through natural reasoning, one can never take hold of the meaning of Christ's crucifixion. However, to those who become intimately acquainted with the risen Savior through experience, the cross is the power of God manifested. We must take a hands-on approach to the cross. For upon it, God carried the burden of the entire world. In it, we find the support to uphold God's will for our lives because, in the cross, we find our sustenance. The cross gives us the ability to walk the Christian life. God released His powerful resources through the virtue of the cross. As we increase our knowledge of God, we learn through practice that the cross's message is not sacrificing but obedience. Determine to break off any acquaintances with this world system by losing sight of our interests. Through the enablement of the cross, we need to distance our cause from this temporal physical world. We should prove the cross to be authentic by disregarding hell's offerings and rejecting selfish living by replacing it with a selfless life. A banner should be raised high for all to see that the elevated Christ reigns and rules in our lives as we follow the One who preceded us.

We accompany Jesus to the cross, not as an atonement for our sins, but by choosing to become His pupils. Every time we take matters into our own hands and attempt to decide our destinies apart from God's will, it is like coming down from the cross and reviving our crucified sinful life. Jesus easily could have come down from the cross; to die on our behalf was not a requirement; He chose to. He could have distanced Himself from His creation and allowed us to die in our sins by calling down hoards of divine beings to destroy the world to set Him free. Instead, He died a martyr's death for you and me. If you desire wisdom, if you wish to become a spiritually discerning person, you must understand the meaning of Christ's crucifixion. For in it, the glory of God shines from the beginning of time and throughout eternity.

We should pronounce this glory for all to see that we esteem the cross's message of the highest regard possible. Its message should rule our decision-making in everyday matters, with its roots drove deep down into the center of our lives. It is painful to die to self. But the glory of living on the other side of the cross is not something we have to wait to enjoy as blessings fill each day. By understanding that intimacy with God is possible today, we can be the force that drives us into His presence. God has discharged His power. We must become familiar with it through intimacy. The cross of Jesus Christ has made it available for us to have a relationship with God. No longer are we slaves to sin to do its service. Jesus nailed dependence on our fallen natures to the cross. At one time, we were without a share of God's economy. Wandering by that which we now know to be wrong—living in violation of the law of God. But now, in the cross of Christ Jesus, we have a bridge that allows us to pass from the forbidden territory into a glorious relationship with Father God Himself. The cross' message is so simple that men of intelligence prohibit its transmission from penetrating their spirits. They have become puffed up in their learning. As if the author of information is too simplistic for their intelligence. A sad thing is for a finite man to think that he has become more intelligent than his infinite Creator. Trapped by their wisdom, they cannot escape the impediment placed in their way. The snare of obstinacy has paved a path to hell for many who cannot imagine the all-powerful motive of God's love. The eyes of the mind must turn from this worldly wisdom to understand that the beginning of wisdom is the fear of the Lord. Man, full of intelligence, has allowed their acuteness and experiences to dim the eyes of their spirit. They form the best-laid plans for their success, not knowing that their skills and expertise have trapped them.

The cross is the essence of salvation. It is at the cross that Jesus paid the price for the sins of the world. At the cross, Jesus made a public spectacle of the powers of darkness. He took away the ability for the Devil to accuse us judicially by nailing Satan's legal right to rail accusations against the faithful follower of Jesus to the cross. Disarming hell's ability to cast blame on the disciple of Jesus Christ by obliterating the Devil's accusations, wiping them clean off the face of the earth, God has forever erased our sins from His presence. Stripping off hell's advantage, permanently destroying the dominion of sin, He separated us from the power of sin and our union with the fall of humanity. Despite making a withdrawal from the deposits of hell, the sin debt, which we endorsed with our pen, God raised us, elevating us to holy ground, by lifting Jesus and placing on Him the payment of our sin as He hung on the cross of our salvation.

Our souls' liberty from the imprisonment of hell's devices is genuinely the most blessed experience in existence. And it is available to every person on earth. Because Jesus, being God, became a man and shared in natural man's affairs, yet without sin, He could offer a sacrifice for our sins acceptable to Father God. He destroyed the power of death and hell by dying for our sins. There was a time when wrong choices separated all of humanity from God. We were enemies of God, and the thoughts of our minds were continually evil. In dying on the cross, Jesus has reconciled us back into the proper relationship with God. By offering His sinless human body as payment to God for our sins, man has received redemption from the curse of the fall. We now can withstand our sinful, fallen nature by rendering it dead and crucified, along with its evil desires and passions. Death no longer has any hold on us. Death is not a matter of concern for a Christian.

All followers of Jesus will never die. Sure, our bodies get old and eventually decay. Still, our spirits will live forever, not merely existing forever as those in hell will, but eternally experiencing the life-giving energy of God's holy presence. Forever alive, overcoming death, Jesus destroyed him who had the power of death—defeating him on the cross. The Devil is like an old lion that has worn out his youthful attributes with nothing more than a roar to frighten the true believer of Jesus Christ. When Satan had us murder Jesus, he thought he was defeating the Son of Man when, in reality, he sealed his doom.

At one time, separated from God because of our sins, we hated and opposed God in our minds. We brought perils and hardships upon ourselves because of the power of our evil natures. However, by sending Jesus to die on the cross, God defeated the Devil's hold on humankind and brought us back to our proper state of harmony with Himself. Therefore, Satan cannot call us into account and accuse us when we fail because we have become the aroma of Christ to God. The Devil, utterly detesting everything we do, tries to invoke evil on us every chance he gets. Because of Jesus, we have become blameless. Satan can no longer come forward as our accuser to present his charges against us because Jesus became the curse of sin for us.

The divine vengeance of God imputed to the cross of Jesus Christ declares us not guilty. Even though the cross cost Jesus His life, it is the marvelous thing that has ever happened. Our God is God. To know Him intimately has become available to us because of the cross of Jesus Christ. Awareness of God's love in Jesus Christ is the most beautiful thing in all of creation and is why the almighty God created us. The cross of Jesus Christ's message requires no additional help in its effectiveness to turn a sinner from his sins. Its power turns a sinner into a saint. The cross is where the crucifixion of self occurs. It is the pivotal position of passionate desires. The cross is where we determine our efforts or the efforts of God. It is here where we choose to live or die.

Some feel that the cross is not the only way to heaven, which is a sad conclusion to life's meaning. Some of those who deny the cross are well-intentioned people. People who sincerely believe they will end up in heaven because they suppose God cannot be so evil as to throw them into hell forever. However, the Bible is clear that Jesus is the only gateway to heaven. No ritual or penance can aid you in any attempt to enter heaven outside of the cross of Jesus

Christ. That's why it is so vital to render our evil natures crucified with Jesus. The worldly desires lead to death because everything of this life is useless and gravely lacking to enter heaven's gates. False religions miss the mark in their attempts to live upright or through the human effort to do what only the cross of Jesus Christ can do. Those who choose not to believe the message of the cross will not make it. It pleased Father God to put all that represents the Godhead into the man Jesus (Colossians 1:19). Jesus Christ is the substance of God expressed in bodily form (Colossians 2:9). He established a standard of liberty that measures the stature of fullness obtainable by the natural man (Ephesians 4:20-24).

Unlike Satan, who continually sins with no hope of restoration, we do not have to live a life riddled with sin. We need to understand and apply the cross of Jesus' scriptural principles to our lives and to know the love of Christ, which passes knowable consciousness filled with the fullness of Christ (Ephesians 3:19). The very purpose of Jesus becoming part of His creation was to destroy the Devil's works (1 John 3:8). The world system, ruled by Satan, offers pain and death as its compensation. Those who boast in themselves and their earthly accomplishments confirm they do not understand the cross' message. So boasting about anything other than the cross of Jesus is foolishness. There was a time when our wicked ways seemed right to us. But when a person through faith understands that Jesus offered His holy and blameless life to make a bridge back to God once and for all is divine revelation, at that instant, their name gets written in the Book of Life with ink that hell cannot erase. It set us apart for the sacred service of God through the cross of Jesus Christ.

When Jesus was on the cross dying one of the most agonizing deaths known to man, He could look down the halls of time and see you and me. He saw us responding to Him. He saw us giving our lives to Him. And it brought joy to His breaking heart. Jesus died because of a broken heart. It burst forth in pain and agony because of those who would deny Him. Yet if I had been the only one to respond to His saving grace, He still would have gone to the cross, having despised the ridicule and shame of dying an ignominious death. And His seat always would be in the right control of Father God. The cross of Jesus Christ is such a glorious event that to deny the resurrection of Jesus is to leave Him crucified. When a person turns to Christ and is born again, it reveals the risen Savior's power. If Jesus is not your Lord and Savior, then to you, He is still hanging on the cross, and you make His sacrifice meaningless. Only when a person acknowledges the lordship of Jesus in their life does He come down from the cross on their behalf, taking His seat next to Father God, interceding for them.

Jesus paid the total price for your sins; there is nothing you can add to His payment. There is no other way to get back into the correct relationship with God. The crucifixion of Christ allows us to approach God again. The difference between the Christian faith and other faiths is the object of that faith. To have faith in anything other than the God of the Bible is believing subjective faith itself is the basis of living. The Bible says that Jesus is the front runner of our faith, not the things of this life. He is the One who brings saving faith to a person's life by creating the hope that causes us to increase our awareness of God. It brought joy to Jesus while He hung on the cross to see the travail of His soul, bringing many sons to glory. We should not care what people think when they realize we are Christians. Seated next to Father God, Christ prays for us when we request His help. Of course, we must choose correctly, but God is still a very present help in times of concern.

Christ in Us

The man Jesus was perfect, and the divine Jesus lives in every believer's hearts and minds. Christ in us applies perfection in the believer based on an individual's motives and commitment. Jesus became a man not only to pay for our sins; He became a human so He could understand firsthand what it meant to live a godly life as an ordinary man. He understood the struggles and frustrations that occur in everyday life, which is one reason Jesus said, "My grace is sufficient." God's bounty on present-day living is in the resurrected Christ. A Christian is not liable to fail if he taps into the unfailing strength of God's provision in Jesus, which is inexhaustible, for the weakness of God is stronger than men (1 Corinthians 1:25). That which was inherent in Jesus is available to every believer. For Christ to live in us, we must first die to ourselves. We cannot coexist in our ambitions and follow the will of God. One aspiration or the other must rule in our hearts. To develop a complete understanding of the resource of Christ in us, the hope of glory, we must bring to an end our personal goals in life. The life that Jesus lived is the consummation of integrity and virtue. The completeness of life exists when a Christian realizes we do not live first and die second, but we must die to live.

Life is Jesus; death is the way to find that life, dying to ourselves so we can let Him live in us. A feeble Christian draws from their strength. Bearing trials and struggles in our capacities diminish the working of Christ in us. To be pleasing to God is to lean on His power. The same Jesus who created everything is the same Jesus who lives in every believer. The habitation of Christ possesses our lives. Our weaknesses crucified Him so we could live by the power of God. Because of sin, we are weak; because of Jesus, we are strong. God has chosen the foolish thing of the world to confound the wise, and God has chosen the fragile stuff of the earth to overcome the strong (1 Corinthians 1:27). It is a good thing when we need God to succeed. When wrong springs up and we experience disrespect, we should draw from the wells of salvation to sustain us. When persecution or necessity overwhelms us, we should lean on the power that can keep us from falling. Through redemption, God makes us the habitation of Jesus. He shapes us, transforms us, and makes us completely new through the relationship we gain by faith; nothing can separate us from this love that God has for us (Romans 8:39).

To be in Christ is a relation of restful completeness, as intended in the beginning. It is the life of a new kind, unheard of before the coming of Christ. Gone is the living condition that existed beforehand that used to lead us astray, and we now move forward free from the old worn-out way of living into a fresh way of living not put to use through little human hands. It is divine life engaged through supernatural origin furnished with strength from on high. Jesus died to make us healthy, confirming in us the inherent power of His presence. He qualifies us and supports us with the force and vigor to proclaim His love to a lost and dying world. Christ compensates every individual who gives his or her life to Him with heaven.

However, you need to apply this providential care. When we come to Jesus, we must understand the gospel's message in a saving way before we can clothe ourselves with the garment of salvation. By abandoning the former lifestyle, turning away from the old way of thinking, and turning toward Jesus, renewing our thought processes transforms our minds to an entirely alternative way of thinking. It is completely new, not a refurbished, partially changed form of thinking. We are bound to deposit our old way of living in the grave. A born-again person is like depositing in an empty tomb. Remember death must precede life. Before creating a new life, a corpse must occupy a tomb. Any attempt to hang onto the old living methods is like a person trying to live life six feet under in a grave.

Jesus died a violent physical death before eternally crushing spiritual death. The resurrected life of Jesus breaks hell's misery. This life is available to every Christian who, by choice, dies to themselves. Hidden from the plaques of hell's eternal bondage in Jesus Christ, we should allow this indwelling presence of God to produce great faith. It is a great mystery to ponder the miracle of salvation. God, in His infinite wisdom, defied the grip of hell by demonstrating His love through the suffering that Jesus underwent to satisfy the offense of man. Now the expectation of heaven is obtainable. We have confidence in the future event of resurrection life. Christ in us furnishes the ground of anticipation, and we can place our trust in Him because eternal life is something we possess today. We can allow Christ to live through us, putting to death the deeds that bow to this world system as we cease to live for ourselves. Faith in God develops as we abide in Jesus and let Jesus operate in us. Jesus reveals the hidden things of God. We know the highest councils that govern humanity in the man Jesus, who is God's image. The abundance of God enriches the Christian who realize their relationship with Him based on Jesus's indwelling presence. We should sprinkle our view of ourselves, which determines life's perspective, with dignity and grace flowing from the throne of Christ. The consciousness of man is a function of the mind. Let your conscience be your guide is a phrase that can prove very dangerous. The corruptness of a guilty conscience can lead a Christian to compulsion. Only through a relationship with Jesus is our conscious cleaned and purified.

Association with Jesus Christ is how you achieve genuine freedom from the admixture of our fallen nature. Without controversy, great is the mystery of godliness that removes blame through the truth. God became a man confirmed by the Holy Spirit. Jesus changed humanity's course and is now at the right hand of Father God's throne, seated in heavenly places. God Himself paid the price to redeem us and re-establish our ability to honor the Supreme Being. It is love that breaks the grip of hell in our souls. It is God's love and God's love alone that can change a human being's life.

God is a genuinely present help in seasons of trouble. At one time, we lived in opposition to the facts of God and opposed Him in our minds. God, who is rich in mercy and through His great love, came down from heaven and exchanged the penalty for our actions with the acceptance found in His Son. The accomplishment of this great miracle now makes a way to escape every time the Devil tries to trap us. He gives us safe ground to walk on when everything around us is crumbling. Not only are we saved from the coming wrath of hell, but it also protects us from everyday calamities as God intervenes daily in our lives and keeps destruction away from our door.

Ever since Adam sinned, death has ruled in creation. When he deviated from the truth, humanity fell by the wayside. Through his misdeed, sin entered humans as death exercised its kingly power over everybody, leading us like a dog on a leash. Jesus superabundantly proved His superiority and has regained control over His creation. Overflowing with a measure of authority greater than death, we now exercise the most significant influence possible against the forces of evil whenever they attempt to regain control over us. The vitality of Christ in us allows us to live life to the fullest. Sin ruled over us until Jesus came. Now that Jesus has gone back to Father God, the state of being right with God because of Jesus confirms that we have eternal life right now. It is a future hope but a present reality; even though Adam's one sin caused condemnation for all, God redeems every offense because Jesus lives. He has acquitted every sinner who puts their faith in Him. The unfavorable sentence of sin, along with the force of the law, is now ineffective. With its condemning message, corruption had its damnatory ruling placed right back on top of itself because of Jesus Christ. God Himself was in Christ, reconciling the world unto Himself (2 Corinthians 5:19). Jesus has declared us free from the guilt of sin, and faith in Jesus makes us acceptable to God. We solemnly disclaim the cry of sin's grip in our life when faithfulness springs up from within.

Like a dual casket, we are co-buried with Jesus at the point of conversion. Through death, we have become the habitation of Christ. We have become "hidden" in Christ, concealed from the arrows of hell. However, the solitude of Christ in us ceases every time we stick our head up out of that grave and try to revive our sinful state of affairs. Like inventing something that already existed but had yet to occur, the newness of Christ in us produces new, unused realities. Unprecedented and abounding in life, eternal life is the new reality of every earthly person living by faith in Jesus Christ.

The same strength that produced Jesus from the dead lives in every true believer. The compensation of sinfulness is to be absent from God. In Jesus, we have received that which we do not deserve, life in abundance. Present realities changed because of the well of life that springs from within us and will endure eternity. Before Christ, we could not take part in that form of life that is essentially God Himself—restrained because we were born in sin, to take part in God's original pious position. In Jesus, we have been reborn; we have been freeborn. No longer a slave to sin, exempt from the restraining grasp of sinful obligations, we are now free to choose. Now the righteousness of God is in us who no longer live according to our former taskmaster's plan but according to the newness of life from the glorified Christ. Liberty is the freedom to choose in accord with the intended design of God. Free to claim our inheritance and fulfill our destiny in Christ. Like a garment, we carried around in our bodies the death of sin. But when Jesus died for our sins, we took the garment filled with heaviness off and hung it on the cross. We now can put on the Lord Jesus and receive the full compensation of His sacrifice. Right standing with God is a reality because of Jesus, not because of anything we do, but upon the death, burial, and resurrection of the risen Christ who is in us. God is a spirit, the divine Spirit of life. Our nature revives when we experience the abiding presence of God in our hearts through faith in Jesus Christ.

The Word of God reveals the motives of God. What God has promised, He can accomplish. Once they were a mystery, now made clear through the gospel of Jesus Christ, nothing can divide us from the affection of God. Satan is a liar. He will do whatever it takes to keep you from understanding this truth. If you are currently struggling to free yourself from the grips of the father of lies, the entrapment is not eternal. Satan will tell you that God hates you and that there is no way He will accept you. That is a lie. Even if you are currently an active member of a satanic cult, God's love can still set you free from your bondage. The liar Satan wants you to think he has you trapped forever, but there is hope for you if you are still alive.

Jesus is the way, the truth, and the life. Not even my physical body's death is separation from God because faith in Jesus Christ is eternal life. Nothing in creation has the power to keep me from the embrace of God. Extremities of life cannot prevent the affection of God. The influences of hell cannot prevent me from experiencing the love of God. Nothing that has ever happened or will ever happen to me can stop me from sharing the prize of God in Christ Jesus.

God is love. The reality of how much God loves us needs to become truth in every believer's mind. God, who cannot lie, has made us a promise in His Son Jesus Christ. Satan, who cannot be truthful, wants to keep us from this truth. By dying to our selfish desires and living according to the promise, Jesus lives in and through us. Jesus dying for me is the greatest truth that has ever penetrated my soul. I am alive in Christ. Trapped by sin, unable to perform the things created to do, Christ Jesus, through His blood, set me free from sin; now I am the righteousness of God (2 Corinthians 5:21). Not by works of righteousness, which I have done, but He saved me according to His mercy (Titus 3:5). This life begins by assigning a death sentence to sin's rule and functioning in the life that exists because of our faith in Jesus.

With this truth embedded in our consciousness, we should be thankful in every situation because this is the will of God for us in Christ Jesus. Even though we live our lives in this fallen world, we can operate according to the new nature regenerated in us when we made Jesus our Lord and Savior. We now know and understand what acquaintance with God in a very close personal relationship means. We are on the winning side. God's kindness exerted by the actions of Jesus is the gateway to heaven here on earth. There is now no judgment to pass on to the believer of Jesus Christ. The way to escape the damnation of hell is through faith in Jesus Christ. We use the opportunity available to us by regulating one's life because Jesus made a way to escape. By living according to the Holy Spirit's new nature, we silence Satan's accusations and his lies. Even if you feel you cannot escape your body's sinful habits or the wrongful thoughts lying to you, your sinful body is dead because Christ Jesus is in you. Of a surety is the fact that when they crucified Jesus, we died with Him. Our lifeless sinful body has breathed its last breath; it is deceased. Your destitute life has given up the ghost; you are dead to sin. That phrase is a past tense statement. To think otherwise is to listen to the liar.

We can exert the force of heaven against the gates of hell and live in victory. Because we are dead to sin, we now live a life active and full of physical strength that comes from the Spirit of Christ. Jesus ended the limits the law put on our abilities. The power of the law ended at the cross. The condition acceptable to God is faith in the risen Lord. If you believe this to be true, then credited to your account is the righteousness of Jesus. Confidence in this truth is the key to withstanding the lying onslaughts of the accuser. He is always trying to destroy you and is still trying to lie to you to keep you from understanding the love of God in Jesus Christ. If he can get you to think contrary to this truth, he can defeat you in everyday affairs. Jesus died so we could be free, not only from eternal death, but so we could be open to living our lives in abundance. Truth in Jesus allows you to discover the dwelling of your original design in God. God found us not because of the things we have done, but because we have put our faith in the only way to buy righteousness before God, faith in Jesus. Belief in the God of the Bible is the only road to complete the path of life. The Creator's love for us did not leave us in our sinful state as payment for our wrongful choices. He made a way to escape in His Son. Christ Jesus came into the world to save sinners (1 Timothy 1:15). The Son of Man came to seek and to save that which "was lost" (Luke 19:10). Our thought processes should be the same as those thoughts that Jesus had when He walked the earth. Aware of being a foreigner in a strange land commissioned for a purpose and knowing He was God's purchased redemption, His mission was to lead many souls back to the Father. His opinions of Himself were in harmony with the intention of the Father.

It is necessary to stand the test of understanding and learn how to use our minds' intellectual faculties to get the capacity to perceive spiritual truths. Our ability to reason is a process of our soul and cannot absorb spiritual things unless the Holy Spirit governs our thoughts and energizes our human spirits. Like an army marching off to a distant place to do battle, we need to undertake the struggle of our thought processes, for there is one who opposes our new nature. Satan hates Jesus. When we give our lives to Jesus Christ, Satan's hatred towards us is the same hatred for the Lord. He hates the divine nature developed within a Christian's life, wanting to capture our minds and make us captive to his character, which functions according to sin's principles. Desiring to make you his prisoner through deception, he tries to make it look like yielding to his will does not lead to destruction. Subduing you with false charm and beauty, the strong ties of his affections can seize your mind and ensnare you with false devotion and flattery. If he makes your mind his prisoner, then he can bring you into subjection and cause you to live in defeat. His rule is in the lie (John 8:44). Anything that denies the lordship of Jesus is a lie (1 John 2:22).

God approves us. We should line our thought processes up with the Word of God. I thank God through Jesus Christ because I can now serve God with my mind even though because of the fall, I must bring my fallen human nature into subjection daily (Romans 7:25). By obeying the Holy Spirit, we can put to death the deeds of the flesh (Romans 8:5). Because the carnal mind is enmity against God, Satan tries to defeat us by making our minds function contrary to God's will (Romans 8:7). God knows what we have in mind when we do things. He understands the purposes of our thoughts; therefore, when He sees us choosing correctly, Jesus intercedes on our behalf. We must rein in the mainstream of our reviews, silencing the Devil's attempt to fence us in blocking our mind so he can derail us. Our union with Christ makes the councils of God accessible. God's deliberate purpose and affection being properly allowed based on our supernatural relationship with Him through rebirth enable us to break free from this life's captive mindset. Satan tries to instigate and persuade us contrary to God's things, wanting us to resemble the rest of the world by reducing us to the likeness agreeable and suited for his purposes. God admonishes us to function pleasingly with Him by changing our outward appearances based on an inward operation. He performs heart surgery. We receive a heart transplant. The brilliant luster of our outer countenance is a revelation of an inner transformation. It makes us entirely brand new. Not renovated but changed into a new life, living in opposition to the former state of corruption, no longer mindful of our former interests.

Therefore, our accomplishments should be those that Father God desires, unified in one cause, undivided in purpose. Because who has known the mind of the Lord that we may instruct him? But we have the mind of Christ (1 Corinthians 2:16). God knits us together, causing us to agree to prove His love by demonstrating a power that can change the course of life. This power is love, foreign love. Not one contrived through human means. It is a divine love that gives without measure, never requiring a recompense. All God asks for is a willing mind that can accept His love through the transforming power of His grace.

Peace with God is the renewing of our mind's spirit, receiving the impartation of Jesus that makes us alive as He unites our hearts with the Spirit of God. The divine Son brings us into the state of friendship with God by delivering us from the hostility of sin. Not shaken in mind, troubled in spirit or through words, for the day of salvation is at hand (2 Corinthians 6:2). For God has not given us a spirit of fear but of power, love, and a sound mind (2 Timothy 1:7). God reveals His glory through the mind of a Christian that chooses correctly (Philemon 1:14). God has written His law in our hearts and has put His rule in our minds. When we yield to Him, it frees us from the Devil's grasp, and we become children of the highest God (Hebrews 8:10). The only true God. And co-heirs with Christ Jesus, who is in us.

The peace of God in Jesus allows us to rise above our situations. It keeps us from the rage and havoc of strife. Peace thwarts the struggles and urges that invite the evil one's hostile invasions by watching and guarding our hearts through our ongoing relationship with Jesus Christ. This military guarding of our minds exceeds our ability to understand. On our behalf, divine action liberally supplies completeness in His will for us by realizing that fulfillment is knowing Jesus. We received in Christ the ability to live successfully. It is Christ in us. The Creator of everything abides in us. We need only to advance step by step and exercise our rights as children of God. There are no favorites in God's economy. Everyone who yields to Jesus is free from hell's grasp. He whom the Son sets free is free.

The freedom Christ gives us brings glory to Jesus only when we walk in it. The holy calling of God is according to His purpose. You are no accident; God knew you before He created you; He knew you before your mom and dad met each other. You are not something that has evolved into who you are through the processes of time. You existed in the mind of the personal and infinite Creator before time began. In Christ, you belonged to God before you were born. He created you for this purpose, to accept the love of God that is in Jesus Christ. But not all accept Jesus as their Savior. Not all choose to put on the Lord Jesus by making no provision for every individual's sinful desire. It is a choice. The most important decision you will ever make. No one comes to Father God except through Jesus Christ. And you can't come to Jesus unless God draws you to Him. If you feel a tug in your spirit telling you that God is real and Jesus is alive, then the Holy Spirit is drawing you to a personal relationship with God. You are part of a chosen generation, a holy priesthood. You just haven't claimed your inheritance yet. Humble yourself before the mighty hand of God, and He will lift you out of your circumstances and place you in heavenly places.

The testimony of Christ in us is confirmation that God accepts us. God formed the best plan possible, using the best means available. His love. He fulfilled His mission in Himself. We now can approach the throne of God boldly because Jesus has made us not guilty free from the payment of sin. No longer is a troubled mind crying out loud with fright because we know we lack completeness in ourselves as necessary. The victorious Christ causes joy in us because He successfully closed the circle of life by standing in the gap for all humankind. God has marked off a space in our life so He could inhabit us. He now holds the keys to success for every believer: His power. We are the habitation of God. He is forming and shaping us to change us through the transformation of His creative abilities into completeness. The sea of forgetfulness has swallowed up our original sinful condition as God moves us past our failures and into a fresh way of living. In Jesus, God has befriended us and brought us into a friendship with Himself. As the mediator between God and humanity, Jesus has atoned for our sin and reunited God's peace with the irreconcilable condition of fallen man. Dismissing the charges against us by giving Himself as an offering in our defense, He has placed the righteousness of Jesus ascribed to Himself to our account. In doing so, He has given us what did not belong to us and has taken that which we deserved—advocating His actions with the support of the Scriptures, thus persuading us He is the passageway to God.

Who can stop us if the power of Christ lives in us? If God Himself mighty in us proves to all that Jesus is who He said He is, we are sons and daughters of God through faith in Jesus. No longer slaves to sin, we have become heirs of God through Christ from glory to glory. As Christ dwells in us, we become rooted in the same love that led Jesus to the cross, filled with the fruit of righteousness; our cry becomes "For me, to live is Christ and to die is gain" (Philippians 1:21).

It is God who makes us able. He has an abundance in that which is imaginable. He dynamically desires to explode upon the scene of our lives and create unique resources for living. Greater is He that is in us than He that is in the world (1 John 4:4). Christ has redeemed us from the curse of the law, having become a curse for us (Galatians 3:13). He is working in us what is pleasing in His sight through Jesus Christ (Galatians 3:13), who God has sent forth through the Holy Spirit to live in our hearts (2 Timothy 1:13-14). Now to Him who can do exceedingly abundantly above all that we ask or think, according to the (dunamis) power that works in us (Ephesians 3:20), be glory and honor and praise now and forever.

The Blood of Jesus

Ever since the human species began, the Devil has tried to destroy them. After Adam and Eve sinned, God's redemption plan was set in motion. His first act was to clothe their nakedness. The sin of humankind left them exposed and laid bare. Unarmed and disgraced, their state of affairs became shameful, and they became defenseless, with no way to defend themselves from future enemy attacks. From the first time humanity had stuck its neck out, Satan wanted to chop it off to suppress God's plan for humanity. After the fall, man's condition became incurable and desperately weak, headed for woeful wickedness unless God, rich in mercy, intervened. The first sin of humanity required the shedding of blood to cover it up. God clothed Adam and Eve with the skin of an animal. The vulnerable condition of sin causes death. To clothe man, God sheds blood, requiring the shedding of blood to offer sinful man protection.

Evil always comes at a great price. Even now, it affects those we love the most. The price for its labor is pain. It distorts the natural functions of life and produces grief in its wake. Throughout the ages, we have painted Eve as the culprit who instigated the fall in the first one-flesh relationship. However, Adam was equally at fault during the first scene of man. Adam did nothing; he stood by and watched as the father of lies was deceiving his Eve. When he realized what he had done (by doing nothing), it was as if following Eve into her sin was a better option to him than losing her.

How many times have our selfish choices caused pain and changed the perfect will of God for those we love? Adam, by doing nothing, willingly yielded to what he knew was wrong. Satan tricked Eve, but even though Adam knew it was wrong, he kept silent and did not overcome the enemy's attack by the word of his testimony. Instead, he clung to his life and, in desperation, followed Eve instead of leading her. Man of God, it is time to take the lead and stand up for your loved ones as the blood of Jesus covers us and makes us overcomers. If we abide in Christ, yield our rights to Him, and not cling to what we can't hold on to anyway, then God makes us conquerors. We are overcomers because of Jesus. The execution of Jesus proved Him faithful, and now we are hidden, protected from Satan's attacks.

The blood of Jesus is superior, victorious, and has conquered and subdued Satan. Jesus overcame the Devil by the blood of His sinless sacrifice, now credited to our account. With conflict and defeat dominating us at every turn, the heaviness of sin makes victorious living insurmountable. We are over-matched when Satan comes at us, and if we try to fight him one on one, we will lose. The blood of Jesus had made us invincible. It is now possible to subdue sin and prevail over the enemy because of His blood. Through His death, He (Jesus) has shown the genuine love of God. As the firstborn from the dead, He has proved beyond the possibility of doubt that the power of God surpasses any force that hell can bring against us and rendering certainty to the mind that God is the dominant power of the universe. The shed blood of Jesus is the foundation of God's power, cleansing the wounds of life. Like washing a dead person and preparing him for burial. The blood of Jesus bathes us from the stain of sin.

Freedom from foreign defilement is a reality to a Christian because of the shed blood of Jesus. It is positional innocence. Redeemed by the stamp of God, we can experience a guiltless conscience. Jesus confirms the authenticity of atonement through His deity, saving us with the price paid by His blameless innocence. Aroused from the sleep of death, gathered together, delivered from bondage, distress, and ransomed from the possession of darkness, Jesus, the worth of excellence, has placed His cloak around us. With His blood, He has released the redeeming river of God. Without care for Himself, Jesus has set the mantle of His favor upon all humanity. Everyone who puts their faith in Him, from every tribe, tongue, people, and nation, receives help from God through the public knowledge of the truth as revealed in Jesus. Jesus, through His shed blood, appeased the wrath of God on our behalf.

The Word of God revealed to man clarifies that the blood of Jesus is the flow from which a relationship with God is possible. This power is the release of His community. Communion with God is joint participation with fellow men. If we say we have intimacy with God and are familiar with His ways but walk in darkness, we lie, and the truth of God is not in us (1 John 1:6). Proof of fellowship with God is the association with other ordinary believers of Jesus Christ. As we make our way through life, we avoid contamination by wickedness through the forsaking of evil and taking part in fellowship as immersion in the blood of Jesus washes us from all sin (1 John 1:7). At one time, we were all dead in our sins, without a share in the affairs of God. The blood of Jesus takes away the offense of sin that violated God's divine law. Walking in uprightness and honoring each other, we appropriate the blood through acts sprinkled with supernatural intervention. Made alive by blood, we function according to God's world order. Not one fabricated in man's mind, but one that flows from the eternal fellowship enjoyed by the Father, the Son, and the Holy Spirit. Glory and honor and praises to the Lamb that "was slain." Blood is thicker than water.

We now have easy access to Father God through faith because we have become aligned with Him as kinship in Christ. This ease of access is not inexpensive. It cost the King of kings His life. God wants to wrap His arms around you and treat you like family because becoming a follower of Jesus purges you from the toxic condition of sin that repelled the Father. The progressive situation that exists in us, freeing us from guilt, results from the washing blood that flowed from the cross. The blood of Jesus has made a way free from obstruction. Anything that creates doubt or uncertainty about our position in Christ is a product of the father of lies. With God's promise in our minds, let us cleanse ourselves from all filthiness of conduct and thought, thus qualifying God's holy power by reverencing His saving ability. Jesus, who brings us close to God, breaks the deception that entangles us. The distance between God and us was once farther than anyone could ever travel. We could not make it back to God because the cavernous divide was too great. Discharging the restraint that imprisoned us, we have received a pardon because of Jesus' shed blood. Christ's blood removes the breach created through the law, and we can now pass it over to life. Ratifying the consciousness of sin, the blood that brought death has given life once and for all. Jesus entered the holiest place for us. He did this so we could have eternal redemption. The prominence of Christ gives us boldness to embrace our liberty and approach the throne of God.

Redemption for the forgiveness of every sin we have committed occurred through His blood. And not only that but for every future sin as well. For salvation is according to the eternal riches of His grace. If His blood saved us when we were God's enemies, how much more will His blood save us now that we are friends of God? Peace with God happens through the blood of Jesus. Protection from past, present, or future wrath is in Christ. He has made us the temple of God. His holy dwelling. In effect, His shed blood makes holiness possible. There is a river whose streams make glad the city of God.

This river flows from heaven. It is the crimson tide of the blood of Jesus that has victoriously ripped sinful man from the grasp of Satan's ploys and given us hope based on the truth of God revealed in the crucified Christ.

The Power of the Holy Spirit

God fashioned us to be like Him. He designed us to resemble Him. When God thought about humankind, He imagined someone like Himself. Someone who would resemble Him not in appearance but someone who would have the substance of His qualities. Not an external likeness, but a similarity of His inward nature. God spoke, and creation came forth. He picked up dust from the newly formed earth, and when His Spirit breathed forth, dust became a living soul. God shaped man from the dust of the ground. He transformed matter into life. Evolution teaches that life originated from that which is not personal. The dust of the earth is terrestrial man's exact origin. However, not the way evolution suggests. Natural selection cannot interpret the basis of the Breadth of Life that transformed matter into humankind's new condition, and we know it as spirit or a living soul because it came from the infinite, personal designer.

God is Spirit. Spirit is where life began. The human species became alive when God breathed into him through the agency of the Holy Spirit. This divine Spirit was there when the first Adam came into existence (Genesis 2:7) and was present when the second Adam (Jesus Christ) ushered in the new dispensation for living. He made the physical body of Jesus (Luke 1:35). When Christ was born, the Holy Spirit combined human nature with divine nature. When we are born again, the Holy Spirit adds a sacred character to human nature. God's Spirit is the agency of this holy life. He was the channel used to give life to the original man, and He is the source of energy that allows man to come to a saving recognition of Jesus Christ (John 3:6, 1 Peter 1:22). Salvation is a progressive condition and a present state. Both of which, through faith, the Holy Spirit begins and sustains. Adam was the first man created in the image of God (Genesis 1:26, 5:1). He was the only man with a spirit that was spiritually alive from inception. He was not born in sin, not born in iniquity. His spirit was living from the beginning. After Adam sinned, all who followed him were born with a soul dead to spiritual things. Adam's son Seth was born after Adam's likeness, not after God's similitude (Genesis 5:3). Sin killed the spirit in man. That is why we do not walk with God in the evening's cool, the way Adam did when he was in the garden of Eden (Genesis 3:8a). His spirit was in tune with the Lord; He was fully aware of the spirit world.

Today, man's spirit is born dormant as far as its relationship with God is concerned. It cannot connect with God because of sin. The spirit world is full of agents who do not align themselves with God. So a person can function spiritually and still be dead in their sins. To operate in the spirit world outside of the Holy Spirit is participation in the domain of darkness. Satan rules the unseen spirit world in its fallen state. God forbids us to function spiritually outside of the life and function of the Holy Spirit. Satan knows this and has successfully subdued the reality of the need for the Holy Spirit's influence as a requirement to live a victorious Christian life. Many churches today omit the work of God's Spirit and think they are functioning correctly. Satan wants nothing more than to stop the work of the divine Spirit in the lives of Christians. Christians who do not perform according to the Spirit's power are of no threat to him. This powerlessness is sad because the Holy Spirit affirms in us His divine nature and spiritual condition that confirms that we are loyal disciples of Jesus Christ (Romans 9:1).

It is the Holy Spirit who declares in us we are children of God. God esteems as sons those made perfect in the life and work of the righteous Spirit. God has placed us in His family. He bent down from heaven and cast our sins aside and set us apart for Himself. He took us into His home when we were strangers and made us one of His own. Father God deserves the highest respect and honors anyone can give. Never should we presume Him to be anything other than God. To call Him Father is the most sacred of privileges granted upon man because He is the powerful and infinite self-existent God. Yet our Father is what He is. His benevolent protection stems from His fatherhood, not from His kingly rulership, as He communicates His love through the Holy Spirit (Romans 5:5), expressing itself in the most selfless way possible, sending Jesus to die for the sins of humanity. God is our "Abba Father" because Jesus died and rose again, because Jesus breathed forth the Holy Spirit upon society when He exhaled His last human breath. God has called humankind back into union with Himself through the Holy Spirit, bringing peace and joy to our spirits, allowing us to possess hope.

The ability to receive the complete supply of God's abundance stems from how we relate to the Holy Spirit. First, the Holy Spirit must indwell us. Then, we must invite Him to have control over our entire being. Thus, protection from hell is contingent on allowing the Holy Spirit to have complete control of our lives. Finally, we must ask Him to make us a dwelling habitable to His presence. Demonic possession is actual. It is Satan taking control of a person. This control can extend as far as the spirit of a person. That's why it is so important to ask the Holy Spirit to possess us: to make us His dwelling place. That's why Satan tries to make Spirit-filled believers seem like they are peculiar. It is the influence of the Holy Spirit that makes Christians able to live the Christian life successfully. He (Holy Spirit) guards us by keeping watch over the affairs of the spirit world. He is the medium that lets us take part in the invisible realm in a way that is acceptable to Father God.

Any participation in the netherworld the Holy Spirit does not engage in is dangerous ground and makes you susceptible to demonic activity. The Holy Spirit takes care of us and keeps us from violating spiritual principles. He opens our spirits' eyes and safeguards us from hell's penetrating influences, allowing us to enjoy a peaceful existence here on earth, free from the struggles and calamities some people might experience. God has called us to take part in the battle for human souls. He has promised us exemption from the rage and havoc that can destroy us. But a state of tranquility stemming from passiveness is not our calling. Assurance of salvation is the state of peace, but being content with our earthly lot and not taking a stand against darkness is not a participation in the blessed state of harmony promised by God. God never promised to take us out of the world and the war over humanity. He promised to provide protection from that which could destroy our souls. Satan can endanger our bodies, but he cannot change the fact that our names are in the Book of Life. The power that keeps you from falling is the same power that created the universe.

Pain, distress, and grief are real. Sickness, loss, and heartache are a part of this life. Virtuous living stems from receiving the implanted Word of God and experiencing the passionate expectation of good that comes from an intimate relationship with the Holy Spirit. It is experiencing heavenly comfort amid earthly wounds. If you want to be effective against the demons of hell, then it doesn't matter what we do on our own; what matters is the function of the Holy Spirit. We must surrender to the Holy Spirit to know the genuine work of God. He sanctifies, purifies, teaches us to love God, shows us how to pray, and equips us for service. Satan wants to lead a Christian away from the abiding presence of holiness needed for the Holy Spirit to function. He wants to make a wasteland of the harvest God has given us.

The Holy Spirit is the one who extends our area of influence and provides a return on God's investment in our souls. He throws us into the midst of life to function among those who do not know God so we can grow with strength and vigor that is entirely new. Repeatedly, His actions generate newness of life foreign to the former corruption that influenced us, a new birth radically transformed into a recreation that wrestles us away from the power of evil (Titus 3:5). The Holy Spirit is the emphasis of holy power transferred to us who believe in Jesus Christ. He is the voice of God. The breath of the highest imparting ability to us. Learn to apply this power so you are not soon cast down in mind or troubled in spirit, for the day of Christ is at hand (2 Corinthians 6:2). God will allow things to happen that will shake us up, so we remain helpful for His purpose. He does this to fulfill His purpose in us, the freedom to experience the indwelling presence of His Spirit, allowing us to speak the oracles of God freely with power from on high.

The Holy Spirit is the power that Jesus relied on while on the earth. This leading of the Holy Spirit was the guiding presence of God that the man Jesus used during His earthly tenure. The Holy Spirit will continually lead you to higher ground, even if you are amid troublesome circumstances right now. The Holy Spirit teaches by accompanying you wherever you go. He brings you to the destination He has planned for you, not by showing you the way but by actually going with you. I remember late one night getting caught behind a minivan bent on obeying the speed limit when the road allowed for much faster travel. I was behind this van for quite a while, unable to pass, and was ready to jump out of my skin when suddenly we came around a corner, and to my amazement, hidden behind some brush watching for speeding vehicles, was the local police. The driver of the van knew this road to be a speed trap. I did not. This van, which I thought was slowing down my progress, actually prevented me from getting a speeding ticket. God's Spirit operates like this. We may think God is in our way, impeding our progress when He is protecting us from some unseen trouble lying just around the corner. Never should we launch out, endeavoring to accomplish our resolve without the guiding presence of God's Spirit.

He is God's comfort made complete. The Holy Spirit's assignment brings you into the full measure of Christ (2 Corinthians 3:18). He makes us a reflection of Christ. His job is to develop you and me and make us like the Son of God. What is your wilderness? Where is your barren place? What region of your life needs living water? Know that if you are there because of God, the intent is your completion. God will never leave you. People will desert you, leaving you alone and destitute, but God's Spirit will never send you out without going with you. He needs to find out through experience what you can genuinely endure for the cross' cause. You might be one of those who deny the presence and person of the Holy Spirit. There might not be any room in your doctrine for Him, but whatever pain pierces your heart, understand that it is the Holy Spirit that brings you the peace that passes all judgment.

If you profess Jesus Christ as your Lord and Savior, it is the Holy Spirit speaking through you (1 Corinthians12:3), establishing the course of conduct that leads you down the journey of life. He never compels you by force. He does not forcefully push you to do anything. Never think that God is leading you to suffer the divine penalty for a minute. This type of devotion is destruction. Jesus paid the price. Restitution for sin is impossible outside of the person of Jesus and the finished work of the cross. The Holy Spirit never suggests you should suffer because you need to pay for your wrongs. This kind of guidance is not from God. Suffering to further the cross is a commitment every Christian should make. But your actions cannot add to the cross, and your activities cannot take away from the cross. Restitution is in Jesus, not by saying prayers, doing penance, or punishing yourself because of your sins. God doesn't even re-member the sins of a repentant sinner. We need no further payment for our sins beyond faith in Jesus (Romans 3:24; 8:32).

Obedience, humility, trust, and dedication keep you committed, but the base of your salvation is faith alone. Because of faith, the promised Holy Spirit reveals (that which has been hidden through-out the ages) the miraculous relationship man can have with God. Based on the finished work of Jesus, we can function appropriate-ly (1 Corinthians 6:11) and observe the requirements acceptable to God by the inner working of the Holy Spirit (1 Peter 1:2). The de-termined plan to set us apart from the penalty of our sin originated before time began.

Never listen to the Devil's lies because God has from the be-ginning chosen you to salvation through sanctification of the Holy Spirit and belief in the truth (2 Thessalonians 2:13b). There is no way Satan can legally come in and condemn a Christian (Romans 8:1) even when they sin and fall short of the glory of God (Romans 3:23). By complying with the Holy Spirit's leading, we cleanse our-selves from the stain of sin and distinguish between truth and error in any circumstance we encounter in life.

Do you want to experience life under your dead circumstances? Then know the handwriting on the walls of hell that condemns you no longer exists in the mind of God (Colossians 2:14). It is a sacred thing to know the saving grace of God, to delineate between life and death. The Holy Spirit produces energy. Not just the ability to breathe and exist, but to understand authentic life. The Holy Spirit has vital living power in Himself, and He imparts it into our spirits. He restored our spirit and made it alive when we accepted Jesus as our personal Savior. He invigorates our lives every single day with an active force that flows from the throne of Father God. The divine Spirit appoints us with the ability to perform as it is He who authors and executes the things ordained for us to do. He is the revelatory part of the Godhead, making known the Father and the Son. It pleases the Holy Spirit to impart unto us the gift of God, delighting in that which affords joy. He desires to show Himself gracious on our behalf. He is pouring upon us the forgiveness freely given to us through faith in Jesus.

The followers of Jesus have chosen not to take part in the violence of sinful man carried away by every wind and doctrine. We have partaken of the Spirit of Life that we might know the things freely given to us by God (1 Corinthians 2:12). Unless the Holy Spirit reveals God to you, there is no way your spirit can perceive He exists. The soul is the vital force that influences the natural characteristics that allow us to communicate with this existence. It examines and judges our course of action based on the investigation of specific data.

In the same way, the Holy Spirit makes known to our spirit the things of God. He does this through spiritual discernment because only Spirit can reveal spirit. That's why when you reject the Holy Spirit, you are turning your back on the deposit of God in your life (Ephesians 4:30). The security of God's stamp of approval is the Holy Spirit of promise (Ephesians 1:13). Whatever you accomplish for the kingdom of God directly results from your relationship with the Holy Spirit and His relationship with you.

The Bible says to work out our salvation with fear and trembling. You accomplish this in the Spirit. Reverence to God cannot exclude the Holy Spirit. To keep from falling, we must take part with the Holy Spirit or, more accurately, let Him take part in our daily affairs. The influential prowess we possess over darkness comes from the Holy One of God. The authority we have that sustains us is the Holy Spirit's ongoing indwelling presence, His dispensation. It is time for the Spirit of God to take center stage. His story is about to undergo a radical change as He takes His proper place in the lives of believers everywhere. He is about to burst upon the history scene like never and forever change how humanity relates to God. The Old Testament documented the emergence of Father God's sovereignty over man. The New Testament proclaimed the coming of the Son of Man. Throughout time, the current events are appropriately and unequivocally the Holy Spirit's cue to take part in creation determined before time began.

After Jesus died, the Holy Spirit became the focal point of God's relationship with humanity. The Holy Spirit has committed Himself to act on our behalf. It is a past tense reality established long before you or I ever came into being. If this were not the case, then "salvation by grace and not by works" would violate God Himself, who accomplished salvation. The Holy Spirit working within man is a confirmation to the interior part of man's soul beyond his conscience, proving to us it is God who works in us to do the will of

His good pleasure. Therefore, because of this same divine Spirit, we can be confident that He who has begun an excellent work in us will complete it until the day of Jesus Christ (Philippians 1:6).

The Holy Spirit gives us internal peace. This peace is not only of mind but of conscience as well. He is the internal evidence of the divine condition that man enters when he puts his faith in Jesus Christ. He is the internal purity of everything we do, producing the inner evidence of the Scriptures' divinity. The Holy Spirit provides proof that we have now become a part of God's inner circle, the wealth of God revealed enlarging our portion of life. Our relationship with the Holy Spirit increases our natural attributes and creates a tendency towards an abundance of spiritual blessings. He is fullness, wisdom, and power, providing God's grace, revealing the glorified Christ, the brightness of God to our innermost being, and the divine presence of God prepared for His children now and forever.

The power that liberates is possible because Jesus sent the Holy Spirit. He is the application of means that crushes Satan and his demons when they rise against us. The refuge and fortress of God rising within us when the weak things of this life oppose us. He is the inner legal and moral defense that allows us to consider ourselves worthy of calling God our Father. He unites us with God and binds us together, thus validating our opinions of ourselves. God has given us no less than a part of Himself to sustain us as we walk out this life. And this portion is nothing less than a part of the kingdom of His great love.

The Holy Spirit can take an empty vessel and fill it to the brim because of Jesus, making it perfect, lacking nothing. He permeates our entire being by flowing through us, furnishing us with the ability to accomplish God's will in our lives. Like a fully crewed ship breaking through the seas' fury, He helps our cargo reach port by maintaining a steady course through His indwelling presence. Through the declaration, He is the one who interprets the things of God, making God known by breathing life into us. God listens to and hears our prayers through obedience to His Spirit. The Holy Spirit reveals to us we are the remnant of God. We are blood relatives of God in Jesus through the Holy Spirit who has made an official dwelling of God in us (1 Corinthians 3:16; 6:19). He has given us the proper sonship position, the uniqueness of our functionality with gifting that comes from on high. He makes us wise, gives us understanding, strengthens our faith, heals us, works miracles, foretells coming events, gives us spiritual discernment, and is the distinction that sets us apart from the world (1 Corinthians 12:4-11). By providing us with the longing desire to please God, He makes us serious towards God's things. He is the down payment pledged by God to secure our path to exchange this world's currency for heaven's surety.

The Holy Spirit imparts His opinions on us and gives us the mind of Christ. He stands with us and keeps us together by introducing the compositions of God that make us whole, circumventing the fraudulent intents of hell, and stands opposed to hell's purpose for us. He runs alongside us and gets right in the way of Satan's schemes, taking hold of us (for God's purpose) because of the faith we have in Jesus Christ. The Holy Spirit is the Master of ceremonies at all deliverance sessions. He is the fountain that supplies the fullness needed to deliver people from the restraints of hell. Restraining hell to prevent them from affecting our actions and volitions as we enjoy liberty. The power to do this comes from the Holy Spirit. He shows the ability of God on our behalf. One person full of the Holy Spirit is more powerful than all the demons of hell put together.

The promised Holy Spirit is the assurance that God wants to bless us (Galatians 3:14). God is not up in heaven with an ugly stick ready to pounce on us every time we blow it. If we do blow it, God is an ever-present help because we are His children (1 John 3:1, 2). Because of our faith in Jesus Christ, we wait for the hope alive in our hearts. Conformity to the divine law of God keeps us from falling back into sin. Our sinful nature wars against our regenerated spirit. They always will oppose each other. Sin will keep us from doing the things we want to do. By following the Holy Spirit, we remain free from the tentacles of sin and death. The result is a life of rejoicing filled with contentment, tranquility, patience, endurance, integrity, uprightness of heart, determination, acceptance, and excellence. These are fruits from the Holy Spirit's tree, which is the nourishment that provides satisfaction.

If the Spirit of God lives in you, then you can walk in obedience to the concerns of God. By offering ourselves up as instruments fit for the Master's use, the Holy Spirit can use us as the seed to cultivate a life for the surrounding people. Don't let yourself succumb to deception; God uses you to promote living energy, or Satan uses you to inflict death. There is no middle ground. You serve something; everybody does. It is just a matter of whether you are freely choosing to help or bound to serve. Everyone has a spiritual vacuum inside of them; you must fill it with something. It's up to you to decide which path you will take, life or death; choose life.

After you accept Jesus as your Lord and Savior, the Holy Spirit of promise fastens Himself to you. The case regarding the destiny of your soul is closed. As the confirmation of salvation, He will abide with you forever. He is not something given to you and then taken away every time you sin. The Holy Spirit is God and cannot tolerate sin. It prevents Him from operating. But He will never leave you or forsake you. You might tie His hands with your actions, but your faith in Jesus seals His relationship with you. Therefore, to cause Him grief is to grieve the One who affirms us unto the day of redemption. To still the passion and emotion stirred up by the Holy Spirit is to stifle the One who provides the skill to accomplish the purpose of God in your life. He is eternal unity made manifest. He makes it possible for us to experience the unity of heaven wrapped in the bond of love that the Father, Son, and the Holy Spirit enjoy.

There is only one hope. Only one calling. Only one body of believers. All of which come into existence through the one and only Spirit of God. He is the estate derived from Father God through the blood Jesus shed on the cross of Calvary to purchase our redemption, making us joint-heirs with Christ. God has disclosed His truth and communicated His wisdom through the allowed agency of the Holy Spirit. We now clearly understand how to exercise through practice the proper judgments that enable us to avoid evil. Because of Jesus, we have access to God through the Holy Spirit. We have become the abode of God. It is the Holy Spirit that reveals this truth. When you read your Bible, always pray that the Holy Spirit will open up the Scriptures and uncover the mysteries of the fact. He is the One who makes the written Word of God active (Ephesians 6:17), who enables our prayers to take effect (Philippians 1:19), and is proof that fellowship amongst believers is the association with the community of heaven.

Absolute truth is spiritual. Only Spirit can reveal spiritual truth. Strength in the inner part of our being results from spiritual truth understood by the soul providing nourishment to the spirit. Indulgence in excess with the offerings of this life prevents the Holy Spirit from filling us. It is the Spirit of God that allows us to communicate with each other in unconditional love. He changes mere words and turns them into the power of God. He pours forth the truth that flows from the lips of God, expressing it through our very terms. Satan tries to keep us wondering, wandering around, and misleading us through error. The imposter that he is, he corrupts through deception and seduction. The sword of truth implemented by the Spirit of truth is vital in slicing up hell's lies as the divine Spirit makes our behavior fit for heaven by restoring our temperament. To prevent damage, He continuously rescues us from danger by restoring us to our senses through sober thoughts. To curb the desires that bring impulses of destruction, He offers encouragement to our being's core by reining in our mental faculties.

The Holy Spirit is continuously working in the lives of believers who have put their faith in Jesus Christ. God is continually pouring out gifts in harmony with His will for us. Tasting the goodness of the Spirit of God and denying His influence is a serious matter (Hebrews 10:29, 2 Peter 2:21). We must remember it was the Holy Spirit that made it possible for Jesus to maintain the course and hold fast to the cross' mission. It was the Holy Spirit that raised Jesus from the realm of the dead (1 Peter 3:18). And it is the Holy Spirit who purges our conscience from finished works to serve the living God (Hebrews 9:14). The Holy Spirit reveals things to us that even angels desire to know. The drive that makes us unique in the eyes of God is simply the miracle of God in us. By choice, we have become right with God. It is a beautiful thing that God has done. Made to have fellowship with God, not to live in sin, was the original design for humans. Hell, which should not exist, exists because of wrong choices that did not have to come into existence. And they still do not have to operate in the lives of a Christian. We are overcomers by God's power revealed through the Holy Spirit, who has been receiving glory for men's deeds since the beginning of time.

In these last days, as God pours out His Spirit without measure, He will receive the glory for the countless souls ushered into heaven during this dispensation. He is truly a miracle worker, keeping watch over us, performing miracle after miracle on our behalf as He connects with us daily. He is furnishing us with the ointment of God, which is stronger than the consuming fire of hell but soft enough to remedy what ails us. The Holy Spirit's assignment is to protect all who call on the name of the Lord. The Holy Spirit, through the truth, creates the firmness of mind that prohibits hell from agitating us to destruction. God causes shaking in our lives, but His shaking will never harm us because God operates according to wisdom principles. Knowing it is inappropriate to injure people. Keep in mind, of course, that God is infinite. And it is our endless good that is the basis from which He operates. God has given us His Spirit. What more could He do? He is the proof in Himself that He has invested everything He could in making us succeed (1 John 4:13).

God's witness is Holy Spirit. God the Father, God the Son, and God the Holy Spirit are one and agree. The man that puts their faith in Jesus Christ is worthy to partake of their oneness. God's truth in His Spirit makes it possible to live for God, destroying the power of hell through the sacrifice of Jesus Christ. Father God sent Holy Spirit to reveal a foreign love that flows from the majesty's throne on high, the One and only true God, the Creator of all living things. God has paid the price for all the sins in our life. Jesus Christ is the same yesterday, today, and tomorrow (Hebrews 13:8). His eternal purpose for us is from the foundation of the earth. Nothing can separate us from the kindness of God in Christ Jesus (Romans 8:38-39); As already mentioned, this includes every sin that we have ever committed and every sin that we have yet to engage.

The Armor of God

The Bible says that God has given us power over the enemy (Luke 10:19). Satan tries to indwell people and poison lives from within. He lurks around, looking for a way to defeat us. If he can't possess us, he observes us from afar, looking for a way to accomplish his goal, waiting patiently for an opportunity. He builds his plan one step at a time and has a far-reaching strategy for us, knowing it usually takes time to set us up. He conceals his motives, peering about and playing the skeptic. When we try to fight him in our strength, we dig a deeper hole for ourselves. Like falling into quicksand, the more we struggle, the deeper we sink. If he can cover us with his intention, then he can squeeze the life-giving breath of the Holy Spirit right out of our resource pool. He tries to keep us isolated, preventing us from reaching out for help.

Confinement is Satan's castle. Restraint is his reward. He tries to keep us in check through operatives of oppression. He does everything he can to prevent us from realizing that we have the power to act upright and to function according to the truth of God's Word. So that, finally, we have the rite of passage in Christ. After that we can behave according to the dictates of conscience, free from Satan's control and his demons. Exempt from the compulsion to sin through God's power, we can trample the enemy under our feet and crush his intentions. To advance successfully and strike a death blow on Satan's will, we must move with wisdom. Fools rush in where angels fear treading. Do not think for a second that we can outsmart or outmaneuver the Devil, for he is a formidable foe whose high places can trample you down if not equipped with God's armor. With the authority of Jesus, everywhere that the soles of your feet lead you shall be yours (Deuteronomy 11).

The weapons of our warfare come from God. We must be persistent in taking back the ground the enemy has stolen. Satan tries to take the joy out of life and derives pleasure from life's perils. His companion is misery, and his friend is dreadful. The infernal powers of hell want the agonies that an unsaved dying person feels to become a constant in our everyday affairs. We must secure our position and know who we are in Christ, who is the head over every power and principality. Satan is actively hostile toward our minds and our bodies, causing barrenness to the soul. He is a disgusting being, causing hatred within the body of Christ by using divisive means. We can deny his fraudulent attempts at deception by executing a judicious stand based on the evidence made clear by the truth of God's Word.

If we stand on God's truth, Satan cannot hurt us. His attempts to do wrong will always turn out for our good if we are right with God. Nothing Satan attempts can hurt us because he is subject to the authority of Jesus. This authority doesn't mean that we do not have to fight for our rights, nor does it represent a pie-in-the-sky reality. It is imperative to realize that you cannot put yourself in neutral and expect to proceed down the protection path. Engagement is mandatory. We must fight the good fight. Satan wants to lengthen the grip of his rulership. He wants to increase his kingdom by cutting off the reign of Jesus in Christians. He stands like the beast he is and beats his chest with intimidating tactics. Knowing his time is short, he lies to all of his followers, never allowing them to know his grip over man is limited. The escalation of his activities is proof that he is approaching the end of his rule and that the imminent reign of Jesus Christ is drawing nearer and nearer.

As Christians, we should conduct ourselves as if the rulership of Jesus is just around the corner. We should put off the obscurity of action that allows Satan refuge and put on Christ, who has delivered us from the power of darkness (Colossians 1:13). We need to let the truth of God sink deep into our spirits so we can surround ourselves with heavenly sustenance. God has given us the tools to implement warfare. We should be busy preparing for battle. With truth, God's power, and complete armor, we should resist this world's evil (2 Corinthians 6:7), denying Satan any grip on our lives got through terror. Satan tries to cause us to fall, then spits in our faces after he grips us with fear. We should not be afraid of anything or anybody. Satan wants us to lie down and roll over without a fight. We need to show the Devil that utter destruction is his lot, not ours. The total loss and ruin of his reign are inevitable. By rejecting the truth, he sealed his perdition forever. Through trickery, he attacks to get us to deny our salvation. Deliverance and preservation are real and obtainable. Jesus showed proof of this ability by dying for our sins.

All-powerful Jesus could have prevented his death. Yahweh incarnate manifested ultimate power on the cross when He withstood the pains of death and stayed the right hand of His power. His victory over Satan on our behalf was His ability to submit to the penalty of our sin. Now He leads a mighty army of light-bearers that will taste success. We should be strong in the Lord and the power of His might (Ephesians 6:10), for it is Jesus who gave Himself for our sins, that He might deliver us from this present evil world, according to the will of Father God (Galatians 1:4). To reveal Him in us, proclaiming His truth.

Satan brings in false brothers to spy out the liberty we have in

Christ Jesus, that they might bring us back into bondage—trying to use the works of the law to get us under the influence of darkness. We have died to the rule that we might live for God. Faith in Jesus, not works of the law, justifies us. Belief in Jesus is the only condition to keep control of our lives. Otherwise, Satan can march right in and freely make us heed his beck and call. Scripture has clearly stated that Jesus has encapsulated us through the promise that is by faith freely given to those who believe. He did this to redeem us from the bondage of the law that we might receive the adoption as sons of God—knowing that man would not follow the law. It was a means of learning, directing us toward the path that leads to life. That, in the full dispensation of times, He might gather in one all things in Christ, both of which are in heaven and which are on earth, even in Him (Ephesians 1:10). God made Him who knew no sin to be sin for us to become the righteousness of God in Him (2 Corinthians 5:21). So rejoice when the sorrow in your life draws you closer to God. For Godly sorrow leads you to repentance. And repentance is the hinge that holds the gate of salvation wide open. Jesus became poor so that we might experience the riches of His glory (2 Corinthians 8:9). We should put on the whole provision of God so we can make a difference because Christ provides the ability to withstand the onslaughts of life and is the power to exist apart from its grasp.

The method of hell is cunning. Deceitfulness is its craft, and trickery is its ploy. Hell will travel a long way to bring its attacks against you. It strikes you when you have your back turned, trying to change your course of conduct by affecting how you feel—attempting to make you decide according to thought processes that, though foreign, seem as if they are your very own thoughts. Satan lies in wait, watching, ready to masquerade as a natural part of life. When he comes against us, our posture should not make us vulnerable. If he finds us sitting, then he can easily topple us. If you are down on your knees (obviously not praying) or, even worse, laying down on the job, you become easy prey. A tree toppled over by a hurricane has a root system without enough stamina to withstand the force waging war against it. Unable to sustain its life without a robust enough support system in place, it loses the battle. God knows this; that's why He symbolizes the battle armor as a requirement to remain intact when the fury of hell rages. He describes the subject of spiritual warfare as an individual bearing the similitude of a fighter with the peculiar qualities surrounding one who is about to do battle.

All of Satan's methods follow a regulated formula. He uses established protocol in pursuing our destruction. The devices he uses in handling the series of actions that proceed from darkness are still artificial means. His warfare is always deception-based. Unlike the godly battle, we fight based on truth; Satan always contrives some fictitious argument against us to displace our walk. That is why God has called us to arms and to prepare ourselves for work. He has given us that which is subservient to the execution of the plans and purposes He has for us. To produce the effect needed for the victory, we use the means God has readily made available. We must not find ourselves destitute of the complete armor of God required to defend our faith correctly.

Whenever I play ping pong, I always take up a cautious position.

I will carefully return my opponent's advances and return the ball to him, making him take a more aggressive posture. Of course, this defensive posture may not seem very useful on the surface. Still, no matter how long it takes, the other person eventually miscalculates and cannot hit the ball successfully over the net. So sometimes defense is the best offense. If you can adequately defend yourself, it does not matter what is attacking you or how long it continues; you will eventually be victorious. Of the seven items mentioned in Ephesians 6 regarding warfare, five are defensive instruments. However, like my ping pong strategy, each of these pieces characterizes offensive postures as well. God wants us to ward off the Devil's attacks so we can become effective in producing works of righteousness. He wants us to create a harvest of souls and not just hang on by a thread waiting for His second coming. It is essential to learn how to use all of our weapons offensively. A gun without ammunition is of little use. Neither is a gun with the wrong ammo. It is imperative to understand the truth behind spiritual warfare principles to take our stand against the powers of darkness.

Learning to stretch ourselves so we can reach out beyond our natural abilities to activate and exert the greatness of God's power is indispensable. Power is the ability to have control over something. It is equally effective in a passive sense. Jesus wielded dominant power when He submitted to death on the cross. In our ability to act and choose, we must adequately use the arsenal of heaven. By thoughtfully considering our course of action, we can exert the divine authority needed to overcome the negative influences around us. God has given us the ability to process our thoughts free from the decay that leads to improper conduct. To maximize their effectiveness, we must acknowledge our dependence on God as He confirms His ability in us. We should never presumptuously exert boldness void of His defensive covering. To remain secure from assault or injury, we must implement the divine weapons prepared to do the task at hand because hell has many perpetrators. They have the power to govern or control an unprotected individual.

It is vital to learn that, as Christians, we are under the control of God. The sacrifice of Jesus purchased the right of governing in our lives on our behalf. Jesus got predominance over us. He alone rules. It is in Him where we find the peace that possesses the power to overcome whatever happens to us in this life. The contest between good and evil is continuous. To Satan, people are objects of accomplishment. He is trying to slaughter people as God is trying to save people, which means we are the Devil's plunder or God's prevalence. To hold on to our victory in Christ, resound the power of the Lord. The way to success is through adequate preparation to do individual hand-to-hand combat.

Nobody is going to leave their house unless they dress correctly. You would not go to your place of employment without acceptable attire. Most public merchants do not even allow you to enter their establishment without wearing shoes or a shirt. A woman will not go shopping without being appropriately dressed. Yet as Christians, as silly as this might seem, we don't give a second thought about how embarrassed we will be when we forget to properly cloth ourselves with Christ, leaving us unprepared for battle while the Devil beats us up. And we wonder why we are facing life through our failures again. Don't let the sun set on your parade. Conceal your nakedness. God has provided the clothing. Clothe your thoughts with words of excellence. Invest in your well-being.

God does not manufacture puppets. We are the ones who must act to receive the victory. Remember, eternal salvation is not the issue. It is a victory in this life. We must keep ourselves from failing by tapping into the vigor of God to remain unharmed, stand ready, prepared for battle. This battle is being waged domestically in your kitchen and at your workplace. It happens in your car, at the market, during a family gathering. It is on the foreign soil of the earth, but it is a battle on familiar ground.

To succeed in spiritual warfare is not mystical. It is the practical application of God's Word to our everyday lives. Don't hesitate or waver when an attack comes. The quality of your life here and now depends on it. Please take advantage of the circumstances in your life before they take advantage of you. We are all in this together; no one is exempt. The wonderful thing about it is we can choose to win. Victory is a choice. Simply put, the right decisions accomplish success.

I sometimes think people reject the notion of salvation by grace because it seems too easy. Imagine you go to heaven and avoid the pain of hell by merely choosing to put your trust in Jesus. Salvation is a choice. To continue to work out your salvation is a series of choices. Choose this day what you will serve. In my house, we choose to serve the Lord.

The Bible likens this spiritual struggle we are in with a wrestling match. Webster's dictionary describes it as "to strive with arms extended, as two men, who seize each other by the collar and arms, each endeavoring to throw the other off balance by tripping him up and twitching him off his center." Though spiritual warfare is not a physical battle, our opponent attempts to seize the most vulnerable areas in our lives. To prevent us from formulating a counter-attack, he tries to throw us around and thus trips us up in our walk in Christ. If you have ever wrestled before, you know that a three-minute match requires enormous stamina and strength. The simplest-looking opponent can have immense vigor and can become your biggest struggle as you attempt to win the meet. It is not brute strength that wins wrestling matches, but the individual who can maintain a constant advantage wins. The one who can hold his position and cash in on any opening he sees his opponent relinquish.

In life, the simplest things can become your biggest obstacle. Satan will never make his intent obvious. He will never tempt you with something that you would blatantly refuse to do. No, he uses things that seem like they are no big deal if you do them. Then, if he gets you to do it, he uses another small thing. Eventually, a pattern sets in, and the Devil comes in with artillery and blows a big hole right in the middle of your faith. Before you know it, you are blowing it constantly and relatively quickly. God did not come to punish us but to save us (John 3:16-17). We may lose a battle, but we will not lose the war. Do not concern yourself with what happens to your reputation when you expose the strongholds of hell in your life. Don't worry about what people might think or say if you bring an offense you have committed out in the open. When Christians repent, it is essential to mention that it does matter who you confess your faults to. Do it in a safe environment and among those who care for your spiritual wellbeing. However, confession is the only way of releasing hell's hold on your life. Don't let sin fester in you. Give up the ground the Devil is seeking to the lordship of Jesus and take back your rightful territory.

Remember, Christians need not that someone should defend them. They stand open and in plain view of God's eternal eye. He sees all and knows every intent. Repent and release the provision of the cross. Its crimson flow cleanses. The high places of our heart need to bow before the Lord, our God, our Maker. For He is our God, and we are the people of His pasture and the sheep of His hand (Psalm 95:7). It may seem like a setback to expose your sin. The Apostle Paul thought it a light thing to consider what others thought. His focus was on pleasing God. Believe it or not, your pastor or Christian friend will rejoice with you because when you confess a sin, the family of God just gets stronger. What does anybody have that they did not receive? What does anyone accomplish that doesn't find its origin in the provision of God? At one time, we were all sinners. We have all fallen short. No one always does good, not even one person (Romans 3:23). Now we are saints saved by grace. So if it is all grace, then where is boasting? It is in the lie. If we received what we deserved, none of us would make it to heaven. It is Jesus that qualifies us. Faith in Christ is the way to the Father.

So because it is not of our own but God who has lavished upon us the unmerited favor that saves us, it is of the utmost importance to make our defense complete by taking advantage of what God has availed to us. The ability a Christian has at his disposal to live a victorious life is the verb form of the noun describing the power God used to create the physical world and everything in it. It has the same root meaning as our word dynamite. Explosive energy making it possible to succeed and, better stated, impossible to fail. Failure is impossible because our success is in the ability that produced Jesus from the dead. Death's grip is powerless against the force of the cross that is working in us who believe. Whether it is your action or skill, your supply or conditioned intent, or through propitious effects of yours, everything that makes you succeed receives energy by the same ability that raised Jesus from the realm of the deceased. Whatever resource Father God has, He gave to you in His Son through the Holy Spirit. He is the immovable object that makes you stand. He is the irresistible force that propels your energies.

The areas in our life that give us the ability to reproduce life-saving faith receive its validation by conforming to the truth that becomes real to us through God's written Word. To consider the value of anything, you must acknowledge the whole of something. The entire Bible must be viewed as one large mosaic to see its intended message. You cannot take formal truth and slice it up without reducing it to mere relativism. The Bible is not a bunch of independent truths spread out amongst its pages but one encapsulated message conveying God's intent when He created humanity. That's why the area we proceed from must be entirely factual. Based on actual reality. Timeless truth free from the outward restraint of culture is the only condition to determine the difference between hell's deceptive tactics and the eternal truth of God.

A correct position before God is approval based on the guiltless one, Jesus Christ. Jesus is the one who places a protective coating around our vulnerability. The body's vital organs, except the brain, are between the neck and the thighs, representing all the vitality that makes living possible. In ancient times, the breastplate covered the body's front; it also covered the back and the sides. It was an outer covering laid over an inner lining. This inner lining was the part that contacts the body. It had to be tailored to fit your specific body structure perfectly. It allowed you to turn or change posture to resist when attacked without breaking the outer protection of the breastplate. In the spirit realm, Christ's breastplate protects everything necessary to function according to Christ's righteousness. The reinforced liberty we have in Christ is like the inner lining, making it possible to live life without the outer armor's rigid restraint. The chain-link fashion, which fastened this garment together, makes the elegant motion possible for us to function in this inner strength. If this internal function didn't exist, it would challenge maintaining the outer garment's protection when confronted by an enemy. You cannot wear another person's breastplate. Like David, when Saul tried to put his armor on him to protect him from Goliath, it did not work because it did not fit; it impeded his progress. You must put on Christ for yourself, as His life is tailormade for you like this inner garment. We need to fasten the protection of God's peace that comes from understanding the gospel's message firmly in the innermost areas of our walk. Nothing can take the place of your very own faith to maintain your right standing with God and His saving grace.

Try to imagine running barefoot across a scorching desert laden with countless jagged rocks as fast as you can for as long as you can. My guess is after a few brief moments, you would come up lame, unable to continue. Your feet would get cut up pretty badly and start bleeding. In this day and age where adults wear shoes almost all the time, the bottom of our feet became exceedingly soft and susceptible to injury much more than when as youngsters we used to walk barefoot all the time. In the preparation, we strap on the gospel of Jesus Christ providing the adult-like protection needed to walk on this earth without becoming a casualty of war.

To receive whatever lies up ahead on the path of life, we must be fit for the task. To run a marathon without proper preparation and adequate equipping of our feet is preparing for failure. In the same sense, we must grip the gospel's message because it is foolishness to those who do not understand, but to us who believe it is God's power unto salvation. The part of our body that comes in contact with the elements of this physical life is our feet. That is where you get dirty if you were to walk across a muddy field. It is here where you would sustain an injury if you walked across an area of thorns barefoot. By adequately protecting our feet, we prevent damage and can proceed on our course.

That is what it is like for our walk in the spirit realm. It is necessary to take with us the Lord Jesus, who went ahead of us and has paved a way where there wasn't a way. He has made a level path for us to walk on. We should bind the truth of Christ under our feet as we seek to experience the peace of God. Like a farrier makes a horse fit for duty, Jesus furnishes us with the gospel of peace to bear up against even the most challenging terrain. Don't let inadequate preparation prohibit you from victory. Don't let Satan forbid you from standing upright by declaring to you any lie that is contrary to the truth.

A tranquil mind based on the knowledge of the gospel is essential for true happiness. God's peace is as real today as it ever will be in heaven. Christ said, "It is finished." He completed the work. The state of being one with God is available right now. Not one in His nature, but one in a relationship. The gospel is the medicine used to heal the patient ill from the lack of truth. Jesus is the door that opens the way for the condition needed to comply with God's ordinances, making faith the protection that prevents the furnace of hell from becoming our inevitable outcome. He is the opportunity of God to shield us from the flaming arrows of agony. The believer's persuasion places him in a position protected from the pestilence that stalks in the darkness.

Be confident in this; if you believe in the Lord Jesus Christ, your faith saves you. And not only you but also your entire household can fall under the protective covering of Jesus Christ (Acts 16:34), who is the authority over every spirit that exists. Demons tremble at the sound of the name *Jesus*. Satan will someday bow down to Jesus. Like a rope or a cable would pull you up out of a deep crevice, faith in Jesus yanks you from the snare of the evil one. It instantly makes you alive with Christ. We need no other evidence other than resting on the authority of Jesus Christ. You can suppress the plaque that destroys through the divine influence of Christ that comes through faith. The heat that can scorch matter to cinders can't touch a Christian who, through faith, puts on the cross' inflammable substance.

Satan launches missiles of destruction towards us all the time. He doesn't care who he hits or who he destroys. He would love you to work all your life trying to figure out how to live in victory for sustenance and still end up without the nutrition needed to defeat him. Christ has delivered us from the evil one once and for all. But we need to equip ourselves with heaven's properties and tear down the strongholds in our lives. I selected this book's title because, to some, the biblical narrative of life is a fairy tale, making Armageddon fictitious. Others think it will be a physical battle against darkness. Though there will be an end-time cataclysmic battle for all the marbles, I believe the actual battle over humanity's souls is in people's minds. The struggle for the eternal destiny of people is warfare executed in a person's mind. The battlefield of Armageddon is the mind. Ever wonder why you could be in the most pious of situations thinking the most caring thoughts when suddenly, out of nowhere, some unspeakable idea flashes right across the horizon of your thought life? Satan is a thought caster. He places thoughts in our minds and then tries to disguise himself so he can convince us we are the ones pondering these ridiculous notions.

The Devil's strikes that pierce our minds' deepest reaches are why God provided a helmet of salvation as proof of the protection a person receives when he puts his trust in Jesus Christ. Hell attacks the mind; protection of the soul requires guarding our thought life. Suppose Satan can seize our minds, and then our bodies are sure to follow. It is at the extremities of our ability to reason that the Devil seeks to inflict capital punishment. If he can keep us from dwelling on the chief cornerstone of our faith, then he can prevent the mind from receiving divine deliverance. The safety of salvation is the protective covering the reason needs to avoid mental suffering and preserve us when dangerous thoughts are lurking around. The enemy will molest. Taking every thought captive unto obedience in Christ takes practice and often meets much resistance. As creatures of habit, evil thoughts can quickly become bad habits. Our minds' paradigms are an entrenched thought process that needs scriptural-based cleansing. Like a large machete used to pave a way through a dense jungle, the Word of God is a fighting tool that cuts right to the core to reveal the truth.

The Bible says God's word can separate our souls from our bodies and our spirits from our souls (Hebrews 4:12), meaning it can identify what and why you are doing what you do. Humans possess a body, a soul, and a spirit (1 Thessalonians 5:23). All three are vitally important in obtaining deliverance to its fullest, as all three influence our outcome. We must align ourselves with what the Bible teaches regarding our makeup. We are spirit beings in a physical body with the ability to think, feel, and choose. Opposing sickness: Christ died for our complete restoration, making our spirit alive by renewing our minds. Proper spiritual alignment is essential to remain constant in our battle against the dark forces waging war against us. The Holy Spirit should govern over our spirit. Our natural spirit should govern over our soul, and our soul should control the mannerisms of our body. Our bodies should always line up with our souls' dictates, our souls should line up with the will of our spirits, and our spirits should line up with the Spirit of God. If this proper alignment gets out of sync, we become vulnerable to unintended consequences. For example, if our body governs our soul's choices or if our soul dictates its intents contrary to our spirit, our spirit rarely conforms to the will of the Holy Spirit.

Prayer

There are spiritual and sensual aspects to our minds. There is a transformation that occurs when a person puts their trust in Christ. We get the sense of Christ. Because of this, we can pray according to His perfect will. When our prayer lines up with what God wants for us, we receive answers. Prayers do not have to be lengthy or require certain formalities. The due measure of your devotion is in its ability to move the hand of God. Praying at the right time, such as eliminating things that are nearing a boiling point and suffering might occur, is very important. Sometimes we feel the prompt to pray about something we naturally would never decide to do. This prompting is the Holy Spirit in you wanting to move on someone's behalf; God wants you to pray for it into existence. Prayer allows you to talk to God. It also stands in the Devil's way and his schemes. Satan can have something planned. Your prayer can stop what he is trying to do. Prayer creates. It causes that which wasn't and makes it real.

Prayer shows inner courage. Some might think it a weak thing to ask for supernatural intervention in their affairs. But to pray is steadfastly continuing, refusing to let the cause of your prayer fall by the wayside. It is taking advantage of the opportunity to move towards God regarding that which is troubling you. It allows you to proclaim for all to hear that your portion in this life is worth the fight. By pressing close to God, you tightly close the door on anything that might move you from your fixed position. By closely adhering to the principle of prayer, you show yourself unmovable to the purpose you are petitioning. You release the working of God's power through prayer and worship. Entering the throne room of God on your knees terrorizes hell.

Prayer can be individually or collectively petitioned: It is the instrument that moves the waves of darkness out of the path of purity. Whatever you need, whatever you want, whatever you lack, take your case to the throne of God in prayer. The One who created the ear and made hearing possible does not let one morsel of our need fall to the ground without compensation. He discharges angels on our behalf all the time. God never sleeps. His gaze is attentive to our every need, ready to respond to our requests. We have not because we ask not. Jesus promised to answer every request that lines up with the determination of the Father.

He wants us to be on the lookout for anything that needs to change or requires divine intervention—assaying carefully all the things set in motion that may influence a presumed predetermined effect. He doesn't want us to remain passively absent from actions that surround us. God does not want us just to hang around doing nothing and presuming that it's God's will if bad things happen to us. God is sovereign, but not all things that happen to us are of God. He wants us to enlist our efforts to gain an advantage over the influences of hell. Satan's will for your life opposes that which God has planned for you. Learn to unite your intentions with the will of God and encounter hell's attacks by fighting back. Embark on undertaking Father God's concerns and making them real in our lives and in the lives of those we love.

The divine Spirit, where all genuine power comes from, is the faithful prayer warrior's posture. The Spirit of God is the most active force in the universe. He is the most potent force available in resisting Satan and his minions. The Spirit of truth is the posture of success, providing the victory that Jesus won on our behalf that engages the grace that Jesus made to be the reality. Glory to God because the Father has delivered everything we need to succeed. He has clarified that He loves us and wants us to fellowship with Him, free from the bondage of this life that can hold us back. Prayer changes things (Colossians 4:12).

Change is a part of God's sovereign plan for us. Volition makes things happen, and our actions are but the manual operation of conduct engaged through volition. God chose, and the composition of life sprung forth. Our selections affect God's design. It is through prayer that God changes things. Don't think for a minute just because God is all-knowing that we cannot exchange the evil of hell's intent for the good of God's provision. That is how God designed it. Be anxious for nothing, but in everything through prayer and supplication, with thanksgiving, let your requests be made known to God, and the peace of God, which surpasses all understanding, will guard your hearts and minds through Christ Jesus (Philippians 4:6, 7).

The Name of Jesus

The name of Jesus emanated from heaven (Luke 2:21). It is a holy name (Luke 1:49). The name of Jesus represents the authority of God (Mark 1:27). It is in rank the highest name, which is above every name (Philippians 2:9). It commands control, respect, and reflects God's interests, showing us the most excellent way to please Father God. The name of Jesus is the way to salvation, for there is no other name under heaven given among men by which we must be saved (Acts 4:12). Our salvation emerges when we call out to Him (Acts 2:21, Romans 10:13).

His name allows us to prophesy, cast out devils (Mark 9:38), do miracles (Mark 9:39), and gives us a righteous man's reward (Matthew 10:41). The name of Jesus provides trust (Matthew 12:21) and enables God's presence (Matthew 18:20), allowing us to receive a blessing. We receive rewards because of the name of Jesus (Mark 9:41). It will enable us to take part in a new language (Mark 16:17), commissioning us to preach repentance and the forgiveness of sins (Luke 24:47) as it empowers us to become sons of God (John 1:12). The kingdom of darkness is subject to the name of Jesus (Luke 10:17). We receive whatever we ask (according to the Father's will) in the name of Jesus (John 14:13-14). The Holy Spirit sent in the name of Jesus (John 14:26) gives us life (John 20:31). Salvation through repentance is in Jesus' name (Acts 2:21, 4:12). Baptism in His name (Acts 2:38) heals us (Acts 3:6). It makes our bodies strong (Acts 3:16), gives us power (Acts 4:7, 10), and empowers us to speak and teach (Acts 4:18). Signs, wonders, and healing come from the name of Jesus (Acts 4:30). We suffer in the name of Jesus (Acts 9:16). It makes us bold (Acts 9:27, 29), washes, sanctifies, and justifies us (1 Corinthians 6:11). We give thanks to God in Jesus' name (Ephesians 5:20). Every knee will bow at the name of Jesus (Philippians 2:10). Everything we do or say should be in the name of Jesus (Colossians 3:17). It separates us from the world (2 Thessalonians 3:6). The name of Jesus is more significant than angels (Hebrews 1:4). We are not to blaspheme the name (James 2:7) that anoints us (James 5:14). His name is the Word of God (Revelation 19:13). He is King of kings and Lord of lords (Revelation 19:16) called up along the side of us to help us.

Jesus pleads our cause through mediation, providing legal defense in the face of accusation. He is the ruler who controls all things through His powerful influence. Pre-imminent in time and space, the last in temporal succession, He remains faithful. Jesus, who is intrinsically belief fulfilled, is the messenger and representative of God, appearing to man as God incarnate. He stands before God's presence as the Messianic Prince, the delegated messenger of God with specific orders. The symbol of strength with political and military force leading by example as the author of salvation. Jesus is the highest example of faith, and as outlined in Himself, the active cause and origin of this creation. Even though He is the most powerful of rulers, He is love. The Father welcomes us because, as a bridegroom, our overseer, and guardian, Jesus makes happiness real. Making us grow, sustaining us, He makes truth transparent and magnificently clear. The One who brightens our life, reflecting the brightness of God, is the captain of our salvation. He precedes us, puts a song in our hearts, and is the foundation of our faith, setting a banner of victory in our life. Descended from above, He is God's elect, holding the holiest place in the heavens. Through anointing, He gives charge to the objects of God in our lives. He draws us near to God.

Urging, admonishing, and encouraging us, He is our comfort. He instructs, advises, and devises a purpose for our lives, making our message persuasive through consultation. As the beloved, He proves Himself to us by allying friendship with man and God. He is the reason for our behavior, the rising and setting of our day giving light to our life, drawing us to Himself, manifesting that which is desirable, pleasant, and precious in God as heaven's open door, the chosen one of God.

Jesus is the faithful might of God lifting a standard for us. The rallying point of our life without beginning or end His persuasion is reliable, executing God's commands. He is the truth in nature through continuous existence: the perfector of our faith, the first in influence and honor. He is the source and foundation of life, the point man designed to lead the way, making the things of God knowable. As the essence of deity, God's splendor expressing the opinions of God, Jesus also represents the Godhead to man. As our authority distinguishing us from the world, He makes us valuable. He is our controlling counsel, our overseeing commander over man's affairs, the author of time and space affecting our natural senses. As the province of creation, He has gained this earth, as His allotted portion holds His place in the most critical influence in design.

The holy One of God, Jesus, overcame death. He is our hope, joy, and confidence of eternal salvation, the mighty and brave author of deliverance. He is the reason we exist. The impression of God stamped out as a man, the ever-existing God who prevails, the Son of God arbitrating life. As Lord of the earth, the Lamb of God decreeing God's will as the prince of peace, He is the absolute fullness of life. Jesus is the active and genuine vigor of God revealed to man. He is the world's light, showing spiritual purity. He is brave, mighty, efficient, and the breath of life, the One we belong to who possesses, owns, and decides all creation's fate, the God who became a human being to share our weaknesses. Our guide and teacher, Jesus, partook of man's threefold nature, possessing a body, a soul, and a spirit. As a kingly public servant, He represents God's holiness, making the distance between man and God passable. Separated from the world, making us part of the family of God, thus championing victory in life. He is the only way to heaven, forming the best plan for us, using the best means of executing His goal of preserving us by becoming the sacrifice for our sins.

He plants us, makes us grow, is the priest of our lives, and is the power of God living in us. Through the force of God, He performs miracles. As our example, He provides the value of living through physical, emotional, and mental healing. The chief leader, led by God's Spirit, is the propitiation for our sins, appeasing God on our behalf. Given for our sins, He is the one who avenges us. Raised and seated at the right hand of Father God, He paid for our sins. He liberates us by becoming the law of God made manifest as the divine law revealed. He is the condition of life acceptable to God, the revelation of integrity, virtue, purity of life, the rock of stability, and the living root system, which sets us on solid ground. With dominion over everything in creation, He gives us level paths for our feet. He is the embodiment of God's saving grace, the effect of consecration sanctifying our hearts and lives; from His holy place, He is the mark of authority in us, the source that germinates everything that lives. Jesus is the second Adam who re-established the relation of man back to God. Though the righteous practitioner died as a slave, we do not have to be slaves to sin. God entrusts us into the care of the One who controls life, commissioned to save the lost and share His life, bringing tranquility to life, the supreme love of God, and uniting man and God in intimacy. He is omniscient, the sponsor of our salvation, the extraordinary act of God manifested, causing the sun to rise and set. As the mouthpiece of God, Jesus is the moral precepts and thoughts of God revealed. Representing the mental faculties of God, He is the reality of God made accessible to man.

What supports the claim of Jesus? How was His life confirmed? Why are we faithful to Him? Because He keeps us. He upholds us by the word of His power, nourishing us, making us stand firm against the tidal waves of life. He is trustworthy. His Word verifies and establishes Him. He is the pillar of support that makes for lasting results. The mention of His name makes all of hell tremble. He is the good news of the gospel, the force of God reduced down to temporalness to sacrifice Himself for our wrongs. As God revealed, He has made an open show of Father God's nature, removing our enmity with God. Showing us the way, He descended to man and ascended to God as the holy One who carried the entire world's sins to the cross. Jesus is the presence and person of God who goes before, behind, and below us. He stands face to face with God, representing us before the Father, making His permanence firm by His grafting in humankind, thus turning the dryness of life into a region of royalty.

He appeared to us as a mere man, not arrayed with splendor at His appearing, considering man's value worthy of His majesty. But we held Him in contempt. The dislike for Him was intense, as it considered Him not worthy of respect, lacking in virtue. Thought to be only a fad whose impact would be but for a short time, we rejected Him. He was familiar with physical and mental pain. He knew what it meant not to be well. We removed ourselves from His presence, thinking He was despicable. We imagined Him to be of no value. Of a truth, He took our sickness upon Himself, dragged away for our pain. We considered Him worthy of the lashings He received as we felt he deserved death. Jesus allowed our actions that nailed Him to the cross to mishandle Him. He weakened Himself so we could become strong. We treated Him as a downcast as we occupied ourselves with His destruction. It was our shame that He experienced on the cross. Defiled because we rebelled, we live because He died. Crushed and broken because we considered perversity a worthy vice, our iniquity and the guilt and punishment are why He died. He experienced discipline to make us complete. He was content to share the penalty for our corruption so we could experience

His peace and tranquility. With each bruise He experienced, we experience health. With each blow that brought Him closer to death, we share life.

Aimlessly, we have wandered from the truth. We have turned our backs on God. All of humanity has distanced itself from God. We have traveled our paths and have journeyed far from the Almighty. God made Jesus intercede on our behalf. Jesus died because of the consequence required to pay the price of sin. He was hard-pressed in every area of His life, humbled beyond belief. Yet, He never loosed one word in retaliation. They took Him to the cross, cut off and destroyed, bound with the cords of our sin, uttering not one word to devalue the worth of His sacrifice. Our sin laid hold of Him, snatching Him from this life to buy our redemption. The restraints that held Him freed us. God, executing His ordinances as a sentence of judgment on Jesus for us. Who can communicate the value of His worth? Who in this habitation called life can understand His worth? Struck down in the prime of life, our sin taking Him from the earth, the marks of His people were His reward in life. He died the death of the criminal that we all are. We experience the wealth of our reality because He died. He who did no wrong suffered wrongfully. The just One who knew no violence died violently from suffering injustice on behalf of the iniquity of us all and died treacherously but without regret.

Delighted at the work of Jesus, God took pleasure in the life that Jesus lived, seeing fit to let Jesus experience the brokenness of sins' penalty. Jesus became weak with the penalty of sin on our behalf. He shared the substance of the sentence, feeling the emotion accompanied by the burden of sin. Jesus, knowing the actual reality of the cost for our sinful ways, knows how we feel when we pay the temporal price for the error of our courses. He saw the result of His action and advanced to the cross, knowing His plan of reconciling us back to God had succeeded.

The humiliation Christ experienced by dying for our sins was entirely voluntary. He went from the highest position in all eternity to one of the lowest physical experience levels possible. He became the offering that alone could accomplish the entire payment for sin, and He satisfied the righteous requirement of the law written about Him. Therefore, God delights in us and prospers us. Accepted because of Jesus, we are honest. God paid the price for the evils of man in Himself. God saw the trouble and grief that Jesus would experience. And as payment for the sins of all humankind, it satisfied Him. Because what Jesus did has turned the hearts of many sons back to the Father. Through Jesus, many deservingly bound for hell are now righteous in the sight of God. God has apportioned for our everlasting life because of Jesus. We know the excesses and abundance of life because of Jesus. We have gained countless blessings because they lay Jesus bare on our behalf. In emptying Himself of this life, Jesus has bridged the gap between man and God. Reckoned a rebel assigned the portion we deserved; He carried the punishment of all the earth to the cross of Calvary. Jesus took the sting of sin upon Himself, encountering death on behalf of the rebellion of all humankind. Now, God has highly exalted Him and given Him the name, which is above every name, that at the name of Jesus every knee should bow, of those in heaven and those on earth and of those under the earth, and that every tongue should confess that Jesus Christ is Lord to the glory of God the Father (Philippians 2:9).

CHAPTER 8:

SETTING THE CAPTIVES FREE

I trust by now the divine Spirit has enabled you to understand how natural the unseen realm is and the fact that we are engaged in spiritual warfare. Also, that the Devil exists and is a force to be reckoned with in the world today. In this war, you have no alternative but to choose a side, as Satan doesn't leave you alone because you ignore him, as his design is to destroy you. This battle, which has no spectators, is won or lost one person at a time. However, it is unlikely that you or I will ever directly confront the Devil. He assigns minions to accomplish his dirty work in our lives. He bases these assignments on their natures, evil bents, and our naturally unpleasant dispositions. Their goal to bind us keeps us from experiencing freedom in Christ and confines us to their wishes with cords of bondage. They want to tie up our feet to keep us from walking in liberty and fasten our hands so we can't reach out to people with the gospel of truth. They attempt to make us feel obligated to our fallen natures as if we have engaged the covenant of lies in an unbreakable stipulation of duty. Infirmity and distress are what they offer. They use powerful influence to force us to wear their persuasions and desire to penetrate humankind's natural functions and restrict the process that keeps humans pliable before the hand of God. Demons try to border us with legal contracts of evil obligations, making us unable to realize that their hardships are unnecessary. However, even if you have sold out to the Devil, it does not permanently bind you to the will of hell. Nowhere in the Bible does it say the Devil's fire is hotter than the holy flames of the Highest God. Regardless of the reason it exists, every cord of bondage cannot withstand the cutting edge of the sword of God's Spirit. No matter who you are or what you have done, God can set you free from the Devil's authority. Regardless of whatever agreement you have made, Satan's "binding" contract is breakable. Though you were not attentive to the matters of God, you cannot invariably sign away your rights. If you reach out to the Most High, negligence or carelessness do not disqualify you from heaven's provision because conditioned subordination to the power of hell must yield to the person and activity of Jesus Christ.

To be in unity with God and take part in this heavenly provision, we must take a firm stance against that which ensnares us by making Jesus our personal Lord and Savior. Most people bound by the Devil are not powerful Satanists, warlocks, or witches feverishly feeding off the powers of darkness. They are ordinary people like you and me who have opened up a door through ignorance, unbelief, rebellion, or other means they cannot close. Many Christians suffer some restraint in their lives because of the hidden motives of hell. It is not shameful to admit the Devil is tricking you and operating in some area of your life. It is to the heavenly Father's glory that we confess our need to apply the power of the cross to some fallen state of being that exists in us. Don't think it weird if darkness is causing you to fail in some area of your soul. To a certain extent, everybody has bowed the knee to the Devil. That is why Jesus came to earth. The question is, once you have developed an awareness of the dealings of darkness, what will you do about it?

If you discover you are not as free as you should be, my Christian friend, rejoice; God reveals this to you. Satan doesn't want you to acknowledge your faults. Jesus came to liberate us, not punish us. The allegiance you have in Christ breaks the bonds that bind. A troubled person is the one that doesn't think he needs Jesus at all. So it shouldn't come as a surprise to learn that those who can admit their need for Christ require a cleansing. Jesus came to set the captives free. Before Jesus, we were all prisoners of the Devil's devices. At one time, the charm and beauty of the evil one seized our affections. But when Christ arrived on the scene, he made hell subject to His authority. In Christ, we can subdue its agony as well because it doesn't have dominion over us anymore, either. We now possess the capacity to dethrone the vanquished devourer.

In Jesus, we are free. Satan no longer has the power to detain us. Jesus has ended the controversy of man's conquest, conclusively removing all doubt of His legitimate lordship settled at the cross. He dismissed the Devil from Calvary's tree, depriving him of the binding force his authority once employed. It removes his rulership, forever overthrown, releasing us from the obligatory burden of bondage his payroll offered. Jesus permanently removed the shackles, dissolving the armor of captivity with His blood. Now we have the same authority to bind the power of hell that Jesus showed when He nailed the Devil's domain to the cross.

God has secured this authority to become the instrument that unlocked the passageway that ushered in a whole new system of living; He has broken open the padlock that hell had on humankind. He has forever stopped the accessibility of the Devil over those who put their trust in Jesus. If you are in Christ and functioning in His power, hell must obey whenever you silence the Devil. If you have surrendered your life to Jesus, then when you order Satan or any of his demons to leave you alone, they must. Jesus has the keys that lock the Devil out, and He holds the keys to set us free. Please don't misunderstand; it is Jesus alone who stops hell dead in its tracks. His authority must adequately cover us when doing battle, or we could end up in big trouble. Satan is a powerful enemy. Only God has the power to force Satan to do anything. He (Satan) governs his kingdom like a homeowner claims the right to do as they please in their dwelling. Like a man's home is his castle, Satan rules over the fallen affairs of this life. The Devil rules the world that lures you, enticing the flesh that befalls you, authoring everything that leads you astray.

I know the Bible says the Devil is only part of our problem. But Satan has made it commonly acceptable to the church that he is only a small part of the problem. I spend very little time contemplating whether he is behind the things that happen to me. However, he is an ever-present danger that is bent on my destruction. Victory over him does not mean we walk around, expecting him to be lurking at every corner. It is just developing his workings' knowledge and undermining his activity before it surfaces.

If I were to ask members of a modern congregation today to raise their hands if they thought they needed some level of freeing from Satan or his demonic forces, most people would not raise their hands. Some in the room would feel insulted that I would even pre-sume such a possibility. If I were to ask those same people if they wanted to get closer to Jesus or if they would do anything in their power to make a closer walk with Jesus possible, I would venture most hands would go up. Why have we purchased the package that says only Devil worshippers or "messed up" people need some level of emancipation from darkness? Victory over the Devil is not human ability but the power of God working through people filled with the power of the Holy Spirit, who is more potent and mightier than all the hosts of hell put together. In Jesus' name and under the influence of the Holy Spirit, we can destroy hell's hold and plunder his goods (Isaiah 49:24-25).

God does not call for us to function out of control but under His control. We must closely join ourselves to God so we can bind the powerful one that seeks to pierce our lives. A mighty gale can cause much destruction if it is blowing out of control. But if you harness and channel that same force, it can become a powerful ally that can provide enormous energy. In the same manner, God has called us to be active for God and be active against hell regardless of the form darkness takes. Jesus came to make sick people sound. Whether it is this world system, our fleshly desires, or direct influences from demons, we are to stand against it in God's power. Not everyone is to fight the Devil directly through some form of deliverance minis-try. We all have specific callings. Those called to children's ministry win your kids; if you're a marriage counselor, save marriages; if you work in the public workplace, extend the kingdom of God by reducing the kingdom of darkness.

Activeness against hell takes on many forms, with none of these forms reflecting passivity. Before God, humility and obedience are both active traits knowing that God has the power (working through us) to extend His kingdom. God requires us to take action through humility and obedience. Both of which do not define us as passive people because passivity is a domain of darkness. In Christ's passion, we must engage and oppose hell.

One way a Christian can fall into the snare of the Devil is through ignorance. Lack of knowledge is primary to the downfall of any army. Learn to know your enemy. Know what he is doing and where he is operating. We win this war one battle at a time. Not knowing your enemy can open up a tidal wave of trouble. There must be some mental picture that portrays our enemy. Lack of knowledge is a preparation for failure. In a narrow sense of the word, experience is a crucial ingredient in defeating your enemy. You must be able to consider how much force we need to win. Get acquainted with the purpose and intent of your foe in your preparation for battle. If you jump when you should have ducked, you are in deep trouble.

Action is counterproductive if not sprinkled with the knowledge required to produce favorable results. The Devil is trying to darken our understanding of the divine. His work ceases when what he is doing becomes visible. He cannot operate in the light. It exposes him. When you turn on the light in a room, where does the darkness go? It just merely disappears because light triumphs over darkness by eliminating it. Even a shadow is light intercepted. A shadow can only exist when something is interfering with the light rays. Eliminate the object of reflection, and light devours the darkness. Just to be clear, if darkness lives in you, it affects your fellowship. Intimacy with God can only exist in the light of truth because the dark separates you from fellowship with God (1 John 1:6, 7). Darkness dulls the senses, numbing the power of understanding by the hardening of the heart toward the things of God. An impenetrable stony heart casts a shadow over your perceptions, causing a dense fog the light cannot perpetrate. The fog must lift before the light can penetrate. Satan tries to keep us in the mist, prohibiting us from realizing that the overcast of our reasoning is not a reflection of reality but lives in our minds because of his deception. He makes it seem like the entire world is walking in the full knowledge of life. A shadow cast by his presence prevents light from shining on its inhabitants' hearts and minds.

Don't think that you are invincible by mistaking a stubborn heart as stamina. Remaining flexible is where real strength lies. We do not know everything knowable. So as the new truth reveals itself, we must change our life accordingly. To be obstinate is to invite sin. As stated many times, sin functions in darkness. Darkness makes it impossible to see, casting a veil over everything that exists. By turning to the light of the gospel, what exists becomes visible. The Devil always wants to deprive you of the illumination that will change your mind. Don't let his obscurity make you ignorant. He lies to everyone, even himself. He refuses to accept that his lunacy has sealed his fate; if he is so intelligent, why did he betray the infinite love of his Creator?

Unbelief, another trap of Satan, is the preeminent spirit applied by Satan against humanity. The greatest of all sins is in this great evil; the unpardonable sin finds refuge in limiting God (Matthew 13:58). It also limits man (Matthew 17:20). The restriction is in the arms of unbelief (Hebrews 3:19). Refusal to believe is the mark of irrational thinking. Its inspiration to withhold the credit because of the name of Jesus is of the Devil. If he (the Devil) can find any sign suggesting that you might shun the warning signs of your faith, he will place just the right thing under your gaze to lead you astray. Belief elevates you to the highest level of affection and care available in this life.

Notwithstanding, if you fly high on the wings of vanity and then soar down from your heavenly seat in Christ, hell's demons love to terrorize you, making you think all you have to rely on is yourself. Vain self-deception is foundational to unbelief. It is drawing a line that creates a border around the liberties of the cross. You must step over the line of suspicion, leaving the lax of luxury that Satan wants to sell you. You can prohibit God's saving grace by choosing not to believe. That's why this obstacle is the most vicious of all hell's vile characteristics. Not trusting Yahweh and straying to the unholy territory of other gods kept the children of Israel from entering the Promised Land. It is a sin of unbelief that prevents a person from participating in the provision of God's saving grace.

However, unbelief does not make God's efforts ineffective (Romans 3:3) because hell's fury will not prevail against the purposes of God. Even though Satan will come in like a torrent of wind, trying to dislodge anything that sets itself in the foundation of truth, a believer gives God glory by not wavering in his faith. Belief is the strength of faith. Faith makes belief stronger. Unbelief is the only thing that can eternally separate you from God (Romans 11:20). If you fall away from God, induced through selfishness by the force of hell, a backslidden Christian must reapply for inclusion into the family of God by putting to death the deeds of unbelief and renailing them to the cross. A balanced life able to acknowledge sin and repent is living proof that God is alive in you.

One can find mercy through repentant acts that find their origin in the saving faith that fosters belief. We were all born with an unbelieving heart. Shut up in our ignorance and withholding the rain of heaven, preventing it from reigning in our lives. Now, being furnished with an unobstructed view of heaven's gate, be careful not to impede the entrance because of distrust. Be cautious to remain intact so that the blessings of God continue to flow. Depart from the hostile spirit of mistrust and take hold of that which has taken hold of us, even our faith. Don't betray the trust the truth of God has revealed. Cry out to the living God to help your unbelief (Mark 9:24). The impossible is doable if we can only believe. The miracle that allowed us to become believers and our faith's inherent power that keeps us saved gives credence to the absolute power of God's saving grace. Therefore, take heed, my brother, lest there be in any of you an evil heart of unbelief in departing from the living God (Hebrews 3:12).

A sure way to enter the wayward path of ignorance and unbelief is disobedience, a willful refusal to obey what you know is right.

Like an obscured road sign, it lets the truth pass right by you un-noticed without letting it take effect, leaving behind in its wake a total disregard for that which sets us free. How shall we escape if we neglect so great a salvation (Hebrews 2:3)? Neglect is a delib-erate lack of doing that we know we ought to do and taking part in the forbidden, knowing the right thing to do and not doing it. By forming an allegiance with darkness, you create a bridge that can only be closed through repentance. God does not communicate as clearly as most Christians would like because often, we do not obey when He speaks. Who knows what blessing we've missed out on or what problems occur because we didn't follow His directives? Will-ful disobedience puts us in opposition to God's will for us. By not yielding to God, we can become quickly subdued by hell's influence and loosen our fixed position for God. That position being seated in heavenly places in Christ Jesus. Even though our eternal salvation is secure, we will have to stand before the judgment seat of Christ to receive according to that which we have done. Even though we shall judge angels, we will face judgment based on our obedience or disobedience at the mercy of the King of kings. The One who obediently relinquished His rights, compensating for our disobedi-ence. That's why we need to lead our sin into plain view for those in authority over us to see.

Confess your faults to your superiors in the Lord. Humble your-self so those who look out for your soul can provide a covering of protection for you. If you refuse to do this, you could end up in a worse state of affairs than you could have imagined. Like a vulnera-ble member in the animal kingdom that strays away from a protecting herd, if hell can isolate and separate you from the flock, you are in trouble. Even though your knowledge of the truth is fundamental, a Christian who goes back to his old way of living might take up where he left off or, even worse, might become more despicable than ever.

People who turn their back on God might not choose to honor it, but they will always know that Jesus is Lord and the Devil is a liar. The problem is Satan wants nothing more to do with you after you turn your back on him other than to kill you. Even if you slide back to your former way of conduct, the deceiver will never accept you back. He wants you to die in your sins. He wants you to slip into eternity in your sinful, backslidden state. Who knows what the fate of a back-slidden person will be? The Bible clearly shows that such a person's end is not correct (2 Peter 2:20). The foundation of salvation is Jesus' sacrifice. If you choose to walk away from God, the Bible says there is no longer a sacrifice for your sin (Hebrews 10:26).

Being eternally secure is the power to understand that the debt registered in the ledger of life is zero because Jesus removed all debits on your account. And because of this knowledge, you live a life worthy of the calling of God. Integrity is the ability to endure the test of time. Someone who can walk humbly before their God in obedience is an integral individual. Such is the person who will darn the halls of heaven throughout all of eternity. God called us, set us apart, held us, sustained us, protected us, and kept us. It is all God and none of us. Our job is to yield to His calling and take up His cause. As He reveals His will to us, we merely choose to follow, as it is the followers of God who will inherit the kingdom of heaven. It is when you decide not to follow that you find the enemy lurking at your door. In doing so, you give ground to the enemy. Many spiritual problems have roots in the past. It is important not to put a band-aid on our issue's symptom and find its source—the root cause of why we do what we do. The Bible talks about extending a place to the Devil (Ephesians 4:27). It is a geographical statement meaning an actual locality, allowing Satan to take up dwelling in some state of your life. We must find the open door and close it.

Have you ever gone through the process of potty training a puppy so your pet can live with you inside your house? I did. Once. I remember lining my entire living room with newsprint to create an environment for the puppy to go potty without ruining my carpet. Eventually, the dog took ownership of a corner of the room and would only mess in that specific area. I could then remove all the newspapers from the room and leave the newspaper in the corner the dog used as his potty place. After a while, I took the newspaper and moved it right outside the back door, identifying this as the place to poo, so the puppy no longer messed in the room. Eventually, he was going outside, and I had successfully potty trained him.

Simply put, proper interaction with the Devil is kind of like this process. Before you are a Christian, Satan is pretty much able to make a mess of your life wherever he pleases. After becoming a follower of Jesus, you lay a protective covering over your life through a foundation of truth that confines the Devil only to those areas of your life that still need cleaning. Further down the road, you figure out where he is messing with you, a specific area of your life that allows him to function. Finally, after identifying that area where his lurking presence lives, you kick him out entirely. You rid yourself of his company by not permitting him to mess in your terrain anymore.

Think for a moment about the reality of becoming a Christian and cleaning up your house but still allowing some area of your life to remain unclean. Think back to the potty training process and the fact that your potty-trained puppy would mess only in the corner of your house where you allowed him to when you put down the newspaper. Now think about the fact that every day he goes to that corner and messes. And you do nothing about it. Day after day, he messes in the same corner of your room. The newspaper may protect your carpet, but after a few days, your entire house is going to stink pretty severely. If you had anyone over, the stench of that corner would permeate the entire household, and they would smell it. Eventually, the awful smell of that dirty corner affects your ability to function correctly. That's how it is for the individual who gives place to the Devil. As a Christian, Jesus' blood protects you so your life (carpet) won't get ruined because you are Christian. On the surface, not going through a thorough cleaning may seem like a trifling matter. After all, you might say I am a Christian saved by faith. But if you don't clean up your entire house, eventually, that area of decay affects everything you do. When you invite people over, they will notice that the whole of your inner dwelling is not entirely clear. That is what the Bible means when it talks about providing a place to the Devil. Regardless of the high rent he will pay you, don't let him become your roommate. It is not worth the cost of allowing him to live in your life. Kick him out. Serve him with his eviction papers. Make him find some other place to take up residence. Make him find someone else's domain to mess up.

We cannot claim true fellowship with Father God and still allow darkness to make a permanent settlement of our life (1 John 1:6). Therefore, put aside the deeds of darkness and put on the armor of light (Romans 13:12). God is light, and in Him, there is no darkness at all (1 John 1:5). Everything exposed by the light becomes visible (Ephesians 5:13). As we bring light to the hidden deeds of darkness and reveal the motives of hell, we let God's light shine because light can have no association with darkness. The night is passing away, and the bright sunshine is already shining (1 John 2:8). Because our residency is in heaven, we are strangers on this earth. Therefore, we must live as children of light.

As light-bearers, we now realize that the Son of God has come and has given us an understanding, that we may know Him who is faithful and we are in Him who is true, in His Son Jesus Christ the true God and eternal life (1 John 5:20). For He has rescued us from the dominion of darkness and brought us into the kingdom of the Son He loves (Colossians 1:13). Called out of the dark, we can see. His presence lights up our path as He accompanies us through the journey of life. God alone is immortal and lives in unapproachable light, which no one has seen or can see (1 Timothy 6:16). Our inner being enjoys a permanent satisfaction not dependent on any exterior influences but the indwelling presence of the light of eternity. Jesus' blood has drawn us into proximity with God. Once you have rid your life of internal demonic influence, hell will still attack you. The difference is the attacks are no longer from within. After you have rid yourself of the inner struggles of torture, it is imperative to fill your house with godly instruments.

If you leave yourself swept clean but empty, the Devil will try to come in with a moving van full of his diabolical furnishings and try to redecorate your dwelling. If he goes by your home and sees a vacancy sign flashing on and off in one of your windows, he will knock at your door, and this time, he won't be alone. No, using the same devices as before, he will go out and get additional agents to help him move in. Can you imagine what it would be like to live in a house where you had many dogs running around messing wherever they wanted without you being able to do anything about it? Every time you cleaned up after them, they would leave another mess in some other area of your house. That's what the Bible says happens to someone who cleans up their house but leaves it unfurnished. We must put the temple elements of God in the place of those hidden things of shame that used to inhabit our home.

Deliverance from the internal struggles of demonic influence is not an arduous task to accomplish. A commitment to a fresh way of living and a change in lifestyle stamped with a novel way of thinking is the most critical part of being a clean vessel. Getting clean is easy. Staying clean is where the battle lies. Expect nothing less than a fight. The grace of God saves us. But grace not sprinkled with the right choices is about as helpful as making the right choices without the grace of God credited to your account. Put no confidence in your ability. Alarmingly, if God doesn't protect us, we are clay pots in a shooting gallery. High regard for the protective coating of humbly praising God is essential. God draws nigh to those who are low in spirit and of a contrite heart and inhabits the praises of His people. After learning how to live correctly, we should always work out our situations under the Holy Spirit's guiding presence.

Because we are free moral agents, it is up to us to enter the arena of God's will, trying to press in with zeal, being eager to suppress hell. We either choose to lead ourselves to victory, or the enemy takes hold of our apathy to show us the way out from the path of truth. The Holy Spirit urges us to live right before God. We should concede our will and fashion our minds to agree with Him by not refusing heaven's invitation to become genuine in our witness through death to the things we think we should be doing. In the presence of all, we should make it understandable that divine order occupies us. With the arrangement of our affairs yielded as loyal subjects under the governing presence of almighty God, who alone is worthy of praise, we must let go of whatever might trip us up. The Devil is always trying to lure us with scented bait. Offenses are Satan's allurements seeking to draw us away from God's protection. One of the most common entryways left open is the capacity to get offended. If we cannot forgive when some offense sticks its ugly head in our face, the enemy will make the wound a window of opportunity. The inability to forgive is one of the most common doors left open.

We cannot afford to partake of the fruit sent forth from the Devil's offensive orchard. God has too much in store for us. Too much

He wants us to do. We should not accept satanic hurt. The wounds of hell take on many forms. Nonetheless, they are gift-wrapped in unforgiveness. When someone doesn't please you, the Devil marches right in and floods your mind with destructive thoughts. He takes the anvil of despair and assails your emotions, attempting to get you to retaliate. When offended, it is essential to care for our responses, knowing God oversees all. We should look after each other, fully aware that there is only one accuser of the brethren. It is imperative to put hurt behind us, not let it lead us. Hurt has caused many not to reach their goal. If allowed to grow, it will reproduce and possibly turn into bitterness. You cannot spend time with anyone and not experience disappointment. The ones you care about and spend the most time with are the ones who will offend you the most. The rough edge of bitterness is wicked ointment when applied as the healing agent to a wounded spirit. Anyone who annoys you might produce a clamor that lets hell prevail. The Devil wants to change the color of your stripes. He wants to stain the garment of purity applied to your life. Abomination is his outer garment; envy and jealousy are his ornaments; hatred is his reward, and unforgiveness is his degradation. So many become shipwrecked because they cannot forgive someone who has offended them.

The pain that accompanies an offended spirit can become a mortal wound. The dressing of heaven is the only way to receive healing. Just like God's unconditional love for us, the power to overcome offense flows from Father God's throne. He heals, makes new, and is the only One who can take a severe injury and heal it so wholly that no scar remains. God can make a tender response genuine. It is crucial to rid ourselves of the waste that ruins. Inner healing stems from tender compassion's natural function, relieving us of the useless baggage of bitterness. If someone is driving you crazy, then do something pleasant for them. I know this sounds illogical. But if you do, you put God's tremendous restoration power in motion. God preserves us by letting us help each other. We reflect on His love when we love unconditionally—not expecting to receive. That's what grace is all about. And my Bible says grace has saved us. So, just like God has forgiven us, we must forgive. Do you know you can forgive sins? That's right.

When someone sins against you, and you do not hold it against them, you have forgiven that person of their sin. By dying on the cross, Jesus paid the price for our sins, making us right with God. If you forgive, you free that person from the susceptibility of demonic attack in that specific area of offense (1 Peter 4:8). To pardon someone who sins against you prevents a root of bitterness from developing. Bitterness devours everyone involved (Hebrews 12:15). You do not even have to know you offended someone to feel the effects of the offense. If someone finds fault with you or has a complaint against you, it could affect your life, whether you are to blame or not. Forgive those who offend you. Fault finding is the root of hell. Please do not allow it to dig deep and take advantage of you. It is not only the grumbling person who gets hurt. Bitterness is an active agent of evil that destroys anything in its path.

The uproar caused by bitterness breeches friendships, causes disdain, destroys, annihilates, consumes, and lays to waste the condition of the souls of those who partake of its evil morsels. The reproach of bitterness wounds the soul by stripping it of the resource that makes the mind and body healthy. It eats you up from the inside out, taking from your storehouse of substance and cashing it in for the decomposing fire of hell intending to bring utter ruin. Little by little, exhausting the soul, making us a barren wasteland. The moment you let bitterness take root, you become susceptible to darkness, which results in misery.

God wants us to love each other and to hate hatred, as it is a man-slayer. It comes from the father of lies. It can only live in falsehood. The foundation of its existence is in the doctrine of devils. The type of hate I am talking about is hate directed at another believer or an acquaintance that has exasperated you. This kind of hatred can blind you to the concepts of God. It is the enemy of loyal companionship. Fellowship with each follower of Jesus is the cord that proves that genuine love exists in a lost and dying world. Genuine love flowing from a believer's life is evidence that we genuinely know God. Or, put more accurately, are known by God. It also allows us to stand fast in the liberty of God that has set us free. If you want to remain free, then freely forgive. Forgiveness makes you exempt from the fate hell has planned for you. The principle of forgiveness is a sure way of sending the Devil packing without letting him take any part of you with him. To give in to bitterness is to disregard the forgiveness of God (Mark 11:26).

God's forgiveness obligates us to release the debt owed by past hurts. The interest that accumulates becomes more significant than the original account. The contract of self-preference that goes along with unforgiveness is more than you bargained. You must absolve your hurt or become betrothed to the adjudication of iniquity. You may justify your pain, but it doesn't make it right, and it can't change what happened. We should not lead others into sin by the mode of living which we choose. Stand in Jesus Christ and forgive. Work to have a clean conscience with God and man. We must understand forgiveness to stand under God's protective covering. Understanding involves developing knowledge of evil spirits' elemental composition and realizing they can influence Christians by booby-trapping the ground they walk on. They attempt to remove the workings of God to the extent of having a measure of control in sections of their life. It is vital to develop the supernatural ability to distinguish between purposes. The ramification of which allows us to know the origin of any energy attempting to influence your life.

Learn to comprehend what is influencing you. You must know if the spirit is from God, man, or the Devil. Develop an acute awareness of the unseen world around you. The invisible realm can control what our natural eyes can see. Discretion is vital when making judgments regarding the unseen world. A semblance of truth often wraps around falsehood. We have a conniving enemy. The scrutiny of spiritual attack makes for a wise defense. A retreat to fight another day is sometimes vital to survival from danger. Distinguish the evil that contends with us and pronounce judgment on the abductors of our souls. Like the eagle, we need to see the slightest of spiritual movement from great distances.

Understanding

Genuine spiritual understanding involves developing a context that evil spirits can influence Christians and that they can undermine God's work in their lives and through their lives. That is why it is essential to study to show yourself approved. Learn proper conduct. By developing an appropriate measure of the jurisdiction in your living areas, you can prohibit the possibility of living an erroneous lifestyle.

Discernment

Discernment is the supernatural ability to distinguish between essences. It is essential to know what is affecting you because, as stated, God, the Devil, or natural means can influence you. Just because someone seems spiritual to you does not mean what they are saying is appropriate. Dark fallen spirits always try to influence people by pawning themselves off as godly (1 John 4:1). Supernatural revelation must pass the test of truth. Anything that denies the lordship of the incarnate Christ is not trustworthy (1 John 4:2). You must critique the fidelity of spiritual revelation to expose the lies that exalt false truth. Curiosity may have killed the cat, but lack of information destroys human lives.

Honesty

Sometimes the most complicated person to be honest with is yourself. If you need to change, then switch. Self often finds it hard to face the truth. It is difficult to face up to failure. Overly spiritualizing situations that merely need a little honesty can obstruct success by not taking responsibility for actions or decisions. God wants the truth, not blame-shifting or denial. Honesty is a reality unmasked and fact revealed, thus breaking the dominance of hell in our life. Agree with God and confess your faults. When you fail in any area of your life, admit it. It is not a crime to make an open declaration of your wrong. The crime occurs when you try to cover up your failures. It is important to remain accountable and confess your sins to someone. Not by arbitrarily spouting out to people who do not need to know. You do not throw your dirty laundry out in the street for all to see. No, you take it to your laundry room and have it cleaned properly. In like manner, we are to confess to those who look after our souls. Many well-intentioned Christians have shipwrecked the souls of brothers and sisters who sincerely want to get their lives right with God by misappropriating the trust placed in them.

Use discernment when revealing your sins. Don't choose a person who makes it possible for you to keep your spiritual autonomy by concealing your sin, by not betraying your confidence. Expose your wrongs. Take them to the spiritual leaders in your life. Let them know what's going on. If their commission is to govern over you, trust their response. Openly acknowledge your faults, and the joy of God will come in like a flash flood. Honor the Lord with honesty, and you will find health for your bones. God's faithful decree is a writ of divorce, a legal separation of sin from our life, removing the dirty stains left behind by our past as he drycleans our inner garment. His continual abiding presence is the promise to everyone who confesses Jesus Christ as Lord. Repent, and you will find the peace that passes all understanding, filling your clay pot to the brim.

The overflow of confession flushes out the emptiness of sin.

Confession

Once you have given your life to Jesus Christ, Satan is always trying to creep back in and take you back. He wants to repossess you by sneaking in and driving off with the keys that lock him out. Arise from the ashes of your sin. Begin the cleansing process. Fervently turn from your evil ways, or else you will regret the result of the impostors' return. Satan is always trying to turn your world upside down, attempting to overthrow you through the recall of your right standing before God. Don't comfort yourself with the regret of your actions. Dissatisfaction lies in the revocation of our sins. Don't become a refugee of the Devil's undoing. The substance that makes us who we are in Christ is an entirely brand new, not refurbished rightness. God, who is not in the recycling business, makes everything unique. The groundwork of which lies in the endowment of repentance.

Contrition is Godly sorrow. It is not lamenting over our wrongs because we have failed. It is grieving because we have pained the heart of God by sinning against Him. The path to perdition is full of the hardness of a core of inflexibility persisting, contrary to God's will, making for a petrified life. The stony substance of sin dissolves through the flexibility of repentance. We move God Himself with such purity that a change of heart turns judgment into compassion (2 Samuel 24:16). He pities His people and stretches forth His hand when harm befalls us. God often judges us, only to stay His hand when His Holy Spirit turns us from our evil ways. The Holy Spirit in you is the essence of Father God Himself. He links us together with Father God in an unbreakable relationship. Repentance is an offering that costs us. It requires us to bow the knee to the King of glory to recognize our lowly state and know our acceptance because of Jesus. Amend the error of your ways to experience the change that allows you to turn back to God. Get out from underneath the power of sin and produce action that appropriates the person and office of Jesus Christ to our account—no longer caring for the old lifestyle by stripping it of its bragging rights. Erase even the slightest hint of sin. And the due measure of relief rolls in as the creativeness of God refreshes the fatigues of sin. The face of God is toward us. An unrepentant heart deprives you of the legal power of the cross. A person unfit for duty because of the disqualifying grip of sin hinders the authority of Christ that keeps hell from claiming you as a prize. The penitent heart renews the reviving power of God as the lowly in heart inherits the riches of heaven. The cloth of Christ is the garment of transparency, letting the rays of heaven pass through your sinfulness. Like a diamond in water, the opacity of heaven renders sinfulness nonexistent in the life of a sinner who repents. You become crystal clear before Father God when you repent of your sin. It is to one's honor to make your misdeeds known. It cures what ails you.

Unrepentant sin does away with God's protective forgiveness and nullifies the sacrifice of Jesus. Salvation is not something you lose, but frustrating the work of God by refusing to repent thwarts the cross' mercy. It is a grave matter to trample the Son of God under your feet by walking once again in sin, with no regard for the mercies of God. When your emotions betray you and long for waywardness, crucify them. Nail your longings for wrongful deeds with the hammer of repentance to the cross of Jesus Christ. Do it in the sight of witnesses. Let others bear witness to your crucified state. Make a simple statement before God and man. To commit knowable sin and then try to hide it weakens your perspectives. You become less capable of drawing a line between your actions. A seared conscience no longer heeds the warnings of the Holy Spirit, as sin leads you astray. The penalty of which is the end of life. We are all deserving of death. Through repentance, we escape judgment. We need to value Christ's sacrifice and turn from our wrongs by weighing the consequence of sin. To insult the grace of God is to make the cleansing blood of Jesus a common thing, stripping it of its recompensing power. Reckon yourselves dead to sin and alive to God. Repent and choose life. Turn from the payment of death. Change the destiny of death that Satan has planned for you. Harken to the cry of the cross. God has formally called us out of the darkness. It's up to us to proclaim the retentive power of salvation; unless we openly repent, our entire being withers away. We need to put our house in order, thus averting the sting of the forbidden fruit. Now is the time to approach the throne of grace. Do not neglect the author of our salvation. Don't let the love of God slip away. Heed the touch of God on your life by devoting yourself to the practices of righteousness. Hone the ears of your mind. Tune in to what God is saying. Don't let the currents of life pull you from the shores of salvation. God has cut a passageway between your sin and His forgiveness, driven by the force of repentance. Repentance steers you through the obstacle course of sin. If you go over the line, you pay the price as God's purse of victory gets exchanged for the treasures of treason. The fullness of which is a storehouse filled with the repositories of hell. Emptiness is its offering. Carelessness is seeking safety in its ruins. Make sure the path you choose doesn't lead you away from your allegiance to the cross. All roads do not lead to heaven. Don't miss the road signs of life by passing over the toll bridge of death. Flee the grip of hell. Shun the corruption of sin. Repent, and the bearing-cloth of Jesus Christ christens you. Declare the name of the Lord with your manner of living.

As mentioned, unconstrained spirits work against you by using information from your past. A spirit can become familiar to you by observing your past conduct. With the ability to monitor humanity's endless generations, an evil spirit can determine what makes you tick. They also can gain an intimate edge over you by knowing the specific habits of your ancestry. Evil spirits may have a resource of information readily available for use against you, but the Lord God has known you before the beginning of time. So give up your right to be the boss of yourself. After all, you cannot sustain yourself beyond this natural life. Restrain your carnal desires and learn how to be led by the divine Spirit as evil spirits are always trying to get you to abandon your affections for God.

Renouncement

Renounce any friendship or devotion that you have with familiar spirits of your past. The act of renouncing is instrumental. It cuts off any joint operation or obligation you have with any demonic presence and severs the practice that allows them to attach themselves to you. Spiritually, it is a declaration of independence. It is saying, "I don't belong to you, and you own nothing in me." Take responsibility for yourself and refuse to follow suit when the demons of hell entreat you. Evil spirits experience gratification if they can make it seem like you are one of their own. They want you to hang onto anything that makes them feel at home. Like a neighbor peering over your fence and into your open window, they will get intimate with your ways if you let them—disaccustom yourself with the things that domesticate evil spirits in your life. Don't busy yourself with insignificant matters that fill the wasteland of wickedness with the trifles of life. Evil spirits are always trying to get you to neglect the critical issues that prevent them from operating. Turn your eyes towards the presence of God. Set your gaze upon those things that let them know you are a follower of Jesus.

Count the cost and cast your vote upward. Fix the value of living on the truth of Jesus Christ. He alone goes before you, stopping the onslaught of hell's afflictions. The God of mercy shall prevent the demolition of darkness from laying waste to your livelihood. The mixture that comes from shameful actions confounds the distinctiveness of truth. God is not the author of confusion. He makes things crystal clear, bringing you to a closer union with Him through the control of His Holy Spirit. He centralizes your energies to get you focused on Him. Don't be afraid to speak out against the rage of hell. Stop it dead in its tracks. Derail the demons that attempt to pour themselves into you or their invisible labors will rush in at the drop of a hat.

Pattern your life after the regulations of intrinsic truth. And the God of peace will show Himself, proving to you He stands with you committed to your success. Every individual must decide. Will you live according to the truth or get caught up in the allurements of deceit? How you handle the revelation of the Son of God decides everything that happens to you. No one expects to be taken out by evil, though it doesn't come by chance. However, the evil that occurs to you doesn't have to arrive. Don't be a fatalist. Jesus changed the course of history by revealing the fortunes of heaven. It is possible to stop bad things that might happen. It may take the intervention of a brother or sister on your behalf—help from a mature believer. But know of a truth that the anointing of God is available to everyone who believes, equipping you to stand in the gap. Greater is He that is in us than he that is in the world (1 John 4:4). We can do all things through Christ (Philippians 4:13), who lives within us. With God, nothing is impossible (Mt. 19:26). He can make you stand. The work, which He has started in you, He will complete (Philippians 1:6). God will accomplish His intended purpose for you. He will remove anything that gets in your way if you renounce the hidden things of shame.

Become desperate for God. Take advantage of the conquest of Christ. He endeavors to keep you from falling. Do not depart from the faith that diminishes the heat of hell. God is everywhere present. He sees everything. His power is greater than the Devil's power. He knows where Satan is, everything he does. Nothing catches God by surprise; there is no panic button in heaven. He is in a state of peace over your life, and from His vantage point, He pours constant blessings over you. Trust in the Lord. Do not lean on your understanding. In all your ways, acknowledge Him. And the God of peace will fill you with joy unspeakable and full of glory. There is a river whose streams make glad the city of God. A flow that increases as we open up the dam of declaration. To pledge your allegiance to the Lord Jesus Christ forbids the Devil from defeating you as his flaming arrows pass over your head as you get down at the feet of Jesus. Make Jesus Lord of your life, and you will realize why you exist (Jeremiah 29:11).

Because of what Jesus has done for us, we owe it to those less fortunate in the faith to assist them in their weaknesses. It is crucial not to repel fellow believers because they do not live up to our standards. Weak faith can cause an error. Help to put back the broken pieces of their past needed to glue them back together. In Jesus, there is not one piece that will remain out of place. Strengthen the fragile believer who needs guidance, not to gain from their mistake but to raise their faith level, helping them walk on their own two feet, so they can bear the cross of Jesus in the strength of their faith. Do not become an excuse for them to wander. Allow yourself to remain approachable to those who do not know better, keeping them from the enemy's lair. It is in weakness that we become strong. Mighty in faith but weak in self-sufficiency. Lead your weak brother by the hand before hell overtakes him. Prevent him from falling by the wayside. Help them mend their ways and reclaim the dignity that comes through rebirth. Help them store up for themself the riches of Christ, always realizing that Satan even has a plan for you if you are not careful.

Caution is prudent for the one who thinks he stands. Hell embezzles, trying to bankrupt you through the use of bogus claims. Because the solicitation of hell cares not who it plunders, be at work spreading the effect of the cross in everything you do. You can defeat the enemy. Profit from the proceeds of heaven. Take ownership of your salvation by acknowledging your wrongs. Avoid the crime of covering up your sin. Through faith in God, His Spirit in you is sufficient. You are not illegitimate but a child of royalty. Perfect in the sight of God. God has set His power in motion on your behalf. The good news is, no matter how afflicted you might feel, God came to tell you about His plan for your life. He has placed Christ over everything to rule over your life to drive the enemy from you. Jesus can heal shattered lives because He satisfied their debt. It is for you that Jesus died. You don't have to stand on the sidelines and watch others enjoy the benefits of God's love. He came to free us all from the oppression of hell.

Restoration brings with it the ability to see clearly. Do not rub shoulders with darkness. Soon, God is going to remove Satan from the scene. He is using the blunt instrument of our earthen vessels to break down the enemy's strongholds. He heals the concussions of hell and quickly reinforces the firmness of our path. Don't let this end of the age deception fool you; the end is coming. God is ushering in the last scenes of this life; it will all be over soon. The tranquil state of God's kingdom will replace the havoc of hell. Are you under the umbrella of God's grace? Is the blood of the Lord Jesus Christ applied to your sin? When this life is over, will God say to you, "Depart from Me, for I am not familiar with your ways"? Or will he say,

"Welcome, My good and faithful servant"? Foreign substances will not take part in the kingdom of God.

Only that which God can become affable with will avoid the eternal flames of hell. He will cast all else into the lake of fire. Remember everything God does is eternal. Where will you spend eternity? Eternally tormented or forever secure in the blessed state of undisturbed peace, free from hell's obligatory agitations? The essence of happiness is peace of mind. Don't let the wars of suffering prevent your mind from choosing freedom. Break free and choose life. Tell the Devil to mind his own business and fix your affections on things above. Your eternal destiny depends on it. The last battle scene of your soul is in your mind. Once again, I ask you, what do you intend to do about it?

If a Christian expects to be ignorant of the Devil and remain free to enjoy the Christian life benefits, they are in for a big surprise. Knowledge is the key to survival. Survey the land or become susceptible to its unknown terrain, ruining your life. Dig up the things that have allowed Satan to take root in your life. You must plow over the area in your life overgrown with the useless sentiments of hell. A brier patch does not yield good produce. Remove any obstacle that will prevent you from becoming useful in every area of your life. Don't leave a part of your territory unusable. Let God come in and bulldoze your life to make it fit for the fruit of heaven. Weed your garden of life. Don't let it get overrun by the wiles of darkness. The root of failure is in the withered work of one who allows his countenance to fade into uselessness. If you don't rise to what God wants to do in your life, Satan will overrun what God intended for you. The Devil wants you to be barren. He wants you to bear no fruit.

Let the revelation of God's Spirit cause you to experience the anointing of living water. Pluck out the evil bent of worldly desires. Remove the inclinations to evil by cultivating the inseparable affections of God's presence. Remove the wild savages of hell, civilizing the labors of heaven. Intelligently exert yourself against the weariness of dry living. God is an enrichment of life. We are to live near the river of living water. Declare the area you call home righteous through the right living justified in your conduct by producing fruit for the kingdom. Become short with evil, impatient with failure, and merciless to the censures of hell. Concede no useable area of your life. Show yourself unwilling to yield and put to shame the blemish of unfruitfulness.

For it is time to experience the fortunes of heaven. Resort to seeking the consultations of God. He will pour deliverance directly into the hollow places of your life. The thorny brambles of hell that used to flourish in the heat of the barren desert will melt away as we rinse the regions of life with the showers of heaven. Let the dew of heaven soak in. Be refreshed by the drizzles of God's presence as they sprinkle on the drought of hell. Cutaway that which prohibits the flow of God's Spirit. The challenging, fruitless areas of your life. Remove the stubbornness that restricts the flow of God's grace and promotes the fierceness of wrath as it kindles displeasure.

Let the river of God's will for you shape your course. Don't dam up the waters of heaven, thus stopping the natural flow of His presence. God has grand plans for you. More than you can ever imagine. Let Him change you from the inside out, setting your spirit free by letting go of what prevents you from falling into His arms. Let Him peel the layers of frustration off by laying aside your earthly cravings and replacing them with the divine influence of His presence so that the things we do are not only lawful but also profitable. Spirit is life. Allow God's Spirit to make your deeds come to life. Only the things of God have any positive effect. Let Him take control of your life. When God tests your life, it's for your wellbeing, as no one can care for you the way He cares for you.

To embrace the oracles of God, you must be pliable enough to recognize the Living Word. You realize that God's written Word thou inspired does not reveal to you that which will change your life unless the Holy Spirit makes it come alive. Discovering the unknown treasures of the Word requires the approved agency of the Holy Spirit. That which the Holy Spirit reveals changes lives. Again, only His Spirit can convince your spirit. Your spirit must become unoccupied with the affairs of hell to experience the touch of God. For improvement to occur, your life must be able to take advantage of the renewing grace of God. It must be land God can possess, land shaken to separate the life-giving fruit from the carcass of dead works.

Cut down that which chokes the life from you. Don't allow things to wrap themselves around you so tightly that you can't shake them loose. Once something has woven a pattern into your life and twisted its way up your entire being, you are in danger of being squeezed to death. Don't let the anxieties of life cause your walk to become fruitless. Let the peace of God restructure your life. That way, you will produce good works. Let Him rend apart the threads that hold you down by penetrating that which is contrary to His working in you. Let us abandon ourselves and let the reformation of God dislocate the infringement of hell's obligations so that we can separate ourselves for fellowship with God. Let God's power disband the influence of sin's suffering, bringing us into a state of openness with God and man. Stop the evil one from penetrating your thought processes and let the dawn of God's presence spring up and clear the fog that prohibits clarity of sight. Endowment with the ability to be free matures that which God has begun. The essence of excellence is letting God's impregnated Word become something more than just written words in a book. Conforming our life to Jesus, the Living Word reveals the model of God's perfect version of man. The all-perfect God was ascribing to man the model for living. Completeness in Jesus Christ. The consummation of maturation, righteousness revealed.

Jesus, the One offered on our behalf to break free of the grip of hell, is the only person who will ever care for you selflessly, the only One who will ever love you unconditionally. All who have your best interests at heart wanting to protect you and keep hell from destroying you are modeling the greatness of God's affection. Choose this day to follow the only way to freedom. The pathway to purity is ripe for the picking. Grab the fruit of the tree of life and ask Jesus into your heart today. Life begins when you let God in; if you do, you will never be the same. If you want heaven's bounty, know that you cannot turn your nose up at God. Satan wants to cut it off and sever all your ties with Jesus Christ because he knows if you make Jesus Lord of your life, you can stop him from making your life miserable. Christ Jesus is God's chosen One. He is the only way to possess life everlasting—the only way to prevent eternal damnation. Ask Him into your life today, and the Devil's power will no longer have a damning influence over you.

Rid yourself of the false things you thought to be true. Remove the thought processes that lead you to believe you needed to add to the saving grace of God for it to cover all your sins. Unnecessary and excessive penance infested with the lying tentacles of hell is not of God. You don't need to be superman to stand before God. All you have to do is break down the barrier of sin through confession and allow the blood of Jesus to wash you white as snow. Learn the evidence of God revealed in His Word. Keep yourself from the forbidden excesses of the wicked. Come down from your lofty place and taste the fruit of humble living. Maintain your posture as a broken vessel before God almighty by casting all your cares on Him.

Keep your mind on Him and experience perfect peace. Jesus is the answer to your world today. He can provide you with an explanation for every one of your questions. As He washes away your past, He will give you present prosperity and establish your future in hope by turning your mourning into laughter. Jesus will take your tears and turn them into joy by planting seeds of rejoicing in your life. He will give you a sure reward if only you will trust Him with your life. Destroy the power of death in your life and accept the love of God. God is the One who keeps the ledger of life. There are things in life you have no control over. If you let God take control of your life, then the outcome of those things is in His hands. He will keep the Devil in check. He will become the arbitrator of what befalls you. Submit to God, and the sovereign rules of freedom will help you bridle the ordeals in life. Don't tolerate the subjugation of hell any longer. Turn your yearnings to God, and the natural areas of your life will fall under the governing rule of the One who controls the universe.

Never forget that Satan only controls that which he can deceive. The truth of the matter is that God is in charge. So the question remains, who is the boss of you? Who or what controls your life? If you are running from God, guess whose arms you are running into. Make your resting place close to the Lord. He is the One who restores broken lives. Taste of what it's like to live in tranquility. The peace of God is more powerful than the fire of hell. If you don't know Jesus as Lord, then the Devil has been pounding on you for years. Do you want to experience a breakthrough in your life? Give Jesus a chance. Why not let God have a shot at you? God promises blessed assurance and offers an absolute satisfaction that won't disappoint you because disappointment is partaking of forbidden fruit. If you lack the strength to carry on, search God out and discover what genuine power is. Seek God while it is still possible. He will listen. Call on Him and find out just how near He is. Then, come home; after all, you belong to the Lord God, not to Satan.

Pursue God and find out what actual life is. He will turn the shadows of your life into the morning sunshine. He will take the dark areas of your life and burst forth with the dawn of His light. Even if you don't care about yourself, God will be gracious to you. He who created everything that exists, who established all the laws that govern science, cares about you. God, who knows you better than you know yourself, is aware of everything in your life. He knows your thoughts, your desires, your needs, all of your shortcomings, and He loves you anyway. He wants to hide you under His loving arms.

There will be a day when God will pour His wrath upon the Earth. Satan's end is imminent. Let God show you how much He loves you. Make the driving force in your life Jesus Christ so you won't have to experience the pain of hell any longer. People everywhere are trying to find the answers for a peaceful living. But, unfortunately, they cannot discover true tranquility because the only gateway to peace is the cross of Jesus Christ. Just like placebos drugs or third-party replacement parts, the Devil has concocted many genuine-looking counterfeits. But he cannot displace the only true God who sat on His throne during Noah's flood and knows the Devil's headquarters' location, making things right in your life by refreshing the areas of your life that need cleaning up. And after He makes things right, He will gently guide you into new truths. Those who reject Jesus are not so fortunate. They will dry up and wither away. Their end will be like a barren desert. As much as God wants to shower you with His love, He can't do it if you don't want it. He will honor your choices by revealing to you His loving influence or, if you so desire, with the abstinence of His sovereign hand. He who commands the clouds to pour rain on all humans cannot help the person who rejects Him. Choose to accept Him, and the floodgates of heaven's provision will open up over you, quenching your thirst. If you let Him in, He will bless your children and your children's children as well. Let the Creator of life pour out His salvation over you. Let him shower His blessings on your home. He wants to communicate with you today. He has planted a seed in your life. Accept God's influences and learn what it means to become more significant than all of your problems. Let the value of humbling yourself before God replace the dreadful guise of arrogance. God is the only One who can give substance to your stature. Everything that does not originate from Him is meaningless when weighed on the scales of eternity. Let the One who renders your life valuable enough to die for it be the one who approves your worth. God loves you so much it hurts. Let Him mend your broken heart. Let Him put the pieces of your life back together. He wants to. So badly that it breaks His heart to see you in pain; choose to accept the dignity you deserve by condemning the damnable deeds of darkness. And become a part of the family of the God who adores you. He will make you blameless in His sight; accept your true inheritance as a child of royalty. Learn what genuine acceptance means. God is seeking you out. He is knocking at your door. Let Him in and know what it means to live.

BIBLIOGRAPHY

Heiser, Michael. *The Unseen Realm.*

Kittel, Gerhard. *Theological Dictionary of the New Testament.*

Morris, Henry. *The Biblical Basis for Modern Science.*

Smith, William. *Smith's Bible Dictionary.*

Thayer, Joseph. *Thayer's Greek Lexicon.*

SCRIPTURAL REFERENCES

All references are from the NKJV of the Bible.

	Acts	1:8, 3:19, 4:8a, 4:12, 4:31, 5:16, 8:7, 10:38, 12:5, 16:16, 17:28, 19:15, 19:18-19, 26:18a
	Amos	5:4, 6, 8, 15
1	Chronicles	21:01
	Colossians	1:5, 9, 13, 14, 16, 20-23a, 24, 27, 29, 2:6, 2:14, 15, 3:3, 5, 8, 11-13, 16, 4:6, 12
1	Corinthians	1:6, 17, 18, 23a, 24b, 30, 2:2, 4-5, 12, 14, 16, 4:11, 19, 5:5, 6:1, 11, 10:13, 12:1-11, 15:1, 31
2	Corinthians	1:10, 2:11, 14, 3:6, 14, 16, 17, 4:2-4, 6-11, 16,17, 5:2, 10, 15a, 17, 19, 20, 10:3, 4, 5, 11:23-27, 12:7, 9, 10, 17, 20, 13:3, 4
	Daniel	3:10a
	Ecclesiastes	11:06
	Ephesians	1:7, 13, 21, 2:6, 13, 16, 3:5, 10, 16, 17, 4:7, 14, 18, 27, 30, 32, 5:8, 9, 11, 19, 26, 6:10-18
	Ezekiel	28:13-17
	Galatians	2:4, 20, 3:13, 16, 26, 4:6, 17, 19, 5:11, 15-17, 22, 24, 26, 6:1, 3, 7, 8, 12, 14, 17
	Genesis	3:18, 5:1
	Hebrews	1:3, 2:1-4, 12, 14, 15, 18, 3:12, 19, 5:8, 14, 6:5, 18, 7:25, 9:12b, 14, 10:5-7, 19, 26, 28, 29, 11:3, 12:1, 2, 13:12, 18, 19, 21b
	Isaiah	14:12-15, 32:20
	James	1:12-15, 19, 21, 3:10, 18, 4:6, 7, 5:16
	Jeremiah	4:03

	Job	1:6-12, 2:1-10
1	John	1:9, 2:1, 14a, 16, 2:20, 3:8, 10, 12, 4:1a, 4, 5:18, 19
	John	1:1, 4:34, 5:24, 38, 8:32, 44, 10:10, 12:31, 14:7, 30, 15:3, 26, 16:7, 13, 33, 17:9, 15, 17, 20, 18:11
	Jude	6
	Judges	7:16-20
	Luke	4:1, 13, 18, 32, 6:18, 36, 8:7, 14, 9:23, 10:21a, 13:16, 24, 14:27, 18:14, 24:49
	Mark	4:7, 18, 19, 6:12, 13, 15:30
	Matthew	3:19, 4:1-11, 24, 5:25, 6:13, 8:16, 28-34, 9:32, 10:1, 12:22, 26, 28, 29, 45, 13:7, 22, 15:22, 16:19, 17:15, 18:18, 19, 23:4a, 12, 25:41, 26:28, 41, 46
	Numbers	22:32
1	Peter	1:2, 3:7, 22, 5:5, 8, 9a
2	Peter	2:4, 18, 20
	Philippians	1:11, 21, 27, 28, 2:3, 5, 8, 12, 16, 3:9, 10, 18, 4:13, 17
	Proverbs	6:12-19, 11:18, 16:18, 18:21
	Psalm	7:14, 19:7, 20:23, 23:4a, 38:20, 40:7-9, 57:1, 71:13, 91:1, 108:6, 109:4, 20, 29, 119:43a, 89, 160a, 126:5, 6
	Revelation	2:9, 10, 13, 3:9, 10, 7:14b, 11:15, 12:4,7-9, 10, 11, 19:13
	Romans	1:13, 16, 21, 30, 3:12, 14, 5:2, 9, 10, 17, 18, 21, 6:4, 6, 11, 22, 23, 7:25, 8:10, 15, 36, 38, 39, 10:4, 17, 11:21, 12:6, 21, 13:1, 12, 14, 14:17, 15:1, 13, 19, 22, 16:2a
1	Samuel	3:22, 49:24, 25
1	Thessalonians	1:6, 2:13, 18, 4:8
2	Thessalonians	1:12, 2:7

1	Timothy	1:9, 20, 3:6, 7, 11, 13, 4:5, 6:1-12
2	Timothy	1:1, 9, 2:9, 15, 26
	Titus	1:2, 2:3, 3:1, 5, 4:5
	Zechariah	3:1-2
	Zephaniah	2:1-3

CPSIA information can be obtained
at www.ICGtesting.com
Printed in the USA
FSHW010731090222
88195FS